An Exorcist Explains the Demonic

GABRIELE AMORTH

AN EXORCIST EXPLAINS THE DEMONIC

The Antics of Satan and His Army of Fallen Angels

Edited by Stefano Stimamiglio
Translated by Charlotte J. Fasi

SOPHIA INSTITUTE PRESS
Manchester, New Hampshire

Cover and interior design by Perceptions Design Studio.

Cover art: "Cross of St. Benedict" (183365198) © serav / Shutterstock.com;
"Concrete wall" (120675925) © Eky Studio / Shutterstock.com

Sophia Institute Press
Box 5284, Manchester, NH 03108
1-800-888-9344

www.SophiaInstitute.com

Sophia Institute Press® is a registered trademark of Sophia Institute.

Library of Congress Cataloging-in-Publication Data

Names: Amorth, Gabriele, author.
Title: An exorcist explains the demonic : the antics of Satan and his army of fallen angels / Gabriele Amorth ; edited by Stefano Stimamiglio ; translated by Charlotte J. Fasi.
Other titles: Saremo giudicati dall'amore. English
Description: Manchester, New Hampshire : Sophia Institute Press, 2016. Includes bibliographical references.
Identifiers: LCCN 2016021936 ISBN 9781622823451 (pbk. : alk. paper)
Subjects: LCSH: Devil—Christianity. Catholic Church—Doctrines.
Classification: LCC BT982 .A4613 2016 DDC 235/.4—dc23 LC record available at https://lccn.loc.gov/2016021936

14th printing

To St. Michael the Archangel

"The battle against the Devil is the principal task of St. Michael the Archangel. And [it] is still being fought today."

—St. John Paul II, May 24, 1987, during a visit to the Sanctuary of St. Michael the Archangel, on Mount Gargano, in the province of Foggia, Puglia (Italy)

St. Michael the Archangel,
defend us in battle.
Be our defense against the
wickedness and snares of the Devil.
May God rebuke him, we humbly pray,
and do thou,
O Prince of the heavenly hosts,
by the power of God,
thrust into hell Satan,
and all the evil spirits,
who prowl about the world
seeking the ruin of souls. Amen.

Contents

An Exorcist Explains the Demonic

Introduction

"In the evening of life, we shall be judged on love [alone]."[1] With this dazzling expression the great sixteenth-century mystic St. John of the Cross expresses theologically the same mysterious reality that Jesus presented to His disciples shortly before offering His life in redemption for mankind. Portrayed majestically by Matthew in chapter 25 of his Gospel, Jesus tells us that each thing we have done, or have not done, to each of the least of our brothers and sisters, we will have done, or will not have done, to Him (see Matt. 25:31–46). Therefore, the last judgment issued on our life will be based on love. Indeed, we ourselves shall reveal the naked truth of our reality to all when we appear before God's presence. This is the heart of Christian life: charity, mercy, and acceptance. At the sunset of our life, all that will remain is that particle of love that we have placed in each thing.

There is, however, another side to this coin: besides being judged on love, we shall also be judged *by* Love, that is, by God. Pope Francis, in declaring the Extraordinary Jubilee of Mercy, has expressed to all the Church—indeed, to the entire world—that the judgment that awaits us is a judgment of mercy. "Mercy will always be greater than any sin, and no one can place limits on the

[1] St. John of the Cross, *Dichos* 64.

love of God, who is always ready to forgive."[2] Each man who seeks repentance and pardon is given the hope that no sin, no situation in life, and no human failure can be excluded from God's love.

This message, laden with hope, is one that I intend to propose and to make my own, together with those who, like me, exercise the priestly ministry of exorcism—those who do face-to-face battle with the devil in order to eradicate his extraordinary action from the lives of men. The enemy of the human race, who rebelled against God and who intends to bring all creation to perdition and destruction, also wishes to make us lose the hope of love and joy in each moment of our lives, including the final moment, when through God's mercy, we shall have restored to us the possibility of redeeming ourselves, after having been separated by original sin from total communion with the Creator. The devil, through his ordinary action, which is temptation, and through his extraordinary action, which is the subject of this book, tries to destroy the confidence of each man and each woman to love and to be loved.

This book, which I have written with my confrere Don Stefano Stimamiglio, began with the desire to fill hearts with the hope that is based on the rock, the Word of God, that neither rain, nor the overflowing of rivers, nor the blowing of violent winds—nor any other dramatic experience from which we could borrow metaphors—can destroy (see Matt. 7:25). It casts light—and I must say finally—on much-discussed topics in the media in recent times: possession, vexation, obsession, and diabolic infestation.

The material we present here has been gathered from our interviews in *Credere* [magazine], published weekly under the

[2] *Misericordia Vultus* (Bull of Indiction of the Extraordinary Jubilee of Mercy), no. 3.

title “Dialogues on the Afterlife.” These weekly installments presented in simple language the elementary concepts of the mysterious phenomenology tied to the cult of Satan and its spiritual remedies. Moreover, they placed these concepts in the necessary perspective of the final judgment of God on men and on history—that is, on the illuminating, salvific events and [the life of] Christ. And so we intend to furnish an essential summary of this topic and to make it accessible to the greater public in all its originality.

I shall begin with a general explanation of the victory of Christ over sin. Then I shall deal with the Catholic doctrine on the fallen angels; the foundation of Satanism, its cult, and its innumerable manifestations; its spiritual consequences; and its remedies. I shall conclude with some fundamental elements of Christian eschatology: the Passion of Christ, His descent into the darkening of Satan, and His return in salvific victory—motives of great hope for all, but especially for those who suffer from the heavy consequences of evil spells, those whom I consider my friends and companions along the journey.

1

The Victory of Christ over Sin and Death

The Incarnation and the Resurrection

Before entering into the heart of the book, I wish to clarify some fundamental truths regarding our Faith and the complex theme of evil spells. Even before speaking of these evils and their author, the devil, and in order to discourage the temptation of sensationalism, I shall put together two fundamental premises that regard Jesus Christ, the Master, the Savior, and the Liberator.

The first consideration regards the profound significance of the Incarnation of the Son of God for each man and woman of every era; that is, the birth of Jesus Christ the Savior, born of the Virgin Mary by the work of the Holy Spirit, which occurred one night more than two thousand years ago in Bethlehem, a small and insignificant locality not too far from Jerusalem. It is precisely this event inserted into the history of humanity that gives us great hope. It is necessary to look at that Baby as the Son of God, who was born in the midst of men and women in order to separate them from sin, egoism, death, and the power of the devil. With eyes animated by faith, one can see lying in that poor stable the Prophet waited for by the people—the Messiah, who, through preaching the Good News of the Kingdom of God, curing the sick, consoling the derelict, and casting out demons, will reveal, definitively, the merciful face of the Father.

The birth of Jesus, however, does not say everything; we must refer to the second fundamental moment in the history of the Son of Man: His death and Resurrection, which we celebrate each year at Easter. The Resurrection of Jesus is the cause of eternal salvation for the souls of those who died before His coming and for all those who came after Him. The Resurrection of Christ throws open the doors of paradise with one condition: that this salvation is liberally accepted by each man. God does not impose acceptance on anyone, and He is always ready to welcome us at every moment.

At the beginning of the Gospel of Mark there are four phrases that summarize the entire work of the Lord and that nurture and give meaning to our existence: "The time is fulfilled, and the kingdom of God is at hand. Repent, and believe the gospel" (Mark 1:15). Analyzing them, we shall understand the sense of the Incarnation and the Resurrection of Jesus.

The first phrase tells us that the time for waiting is finished: from the moment when Jesus is born on earth, He becomes contemporaneously the center of all human history.

Here is the substance of the second phrase: heaven, which had been closed because of sin, is now open, in virtue of the transfigured flesh of Christ in His Resurrection. By now His kingdom of justice and peace has definitively arrived. It is helpful to recall that, according to the Old Testament, the dead had a particular destiny: Sheol,[3] a type of common grave where the Jews believed their souls would end up after death. Sheol was imagined to be a dim, shadowy place that allowed a diminished type of survival after death. It did not, however, liberate man

[3] See Job 10:21; 17:13–19.

from the more perverse and adverse effects of creation: exclusion from perfect communion with God and men. But with the advent of Christ and His Resurrection in the flesh, revelation is now complete: the doors of paradise have been thrown open, and the dazzling light of Christ, raised and living, invades the resting place of all the redeemed.

The third phrase reveals to us that in order to enjoy eternal beatitude, we must change our way of thinking, and therefore our life, in a total and radical way. We have been called to a continuous metanoia, a conversion, a reformulation of the priority of life, so that this reality can also be fully realized in our own existence.

Finally, the forth phrase tells us how to work this conversion: by living the gospel. There we have all that is necessary. The gospel, in turn, summarizes what Jesus commands His disciples: "love one another; even as I have loved you" (John 13:34).

What must we embody in order to assume all of this in a serious way? Permit me to respond with a simple personal anecdote. For twenty-six years—from 1942 to 1968—I went regularly to San Giovanni Rotondo to meet with St. Pio of Pietrelcina. Some of the monks had posters in their cells with inscriptions and reminders. Some were from the Bible but Padre Pio had this: "Human greatness has always had sadness for a companion." The sense of it seemed clear to me: we must have humility, precisely like Jesus, whom St. Paul describes as "emptying" Himself (cf. Phil. 2:7), that is, of making Himself man—even though He was God—and of dying on the Cross, rejected by men. After this poster was stolen from his room, Padre Pio put up another: "Mary is all the reason for my hope." If Mary, who is the Mother of Jesus, is our hope, anyone—anyone who suffers, anyone who is alone, or anyone who feels sad—can look at the Nativity of Jesus and at His Resurrection with a heart full of hope.

The death of Christ throws a penetrating light on our death. The Son of God, making Himself man, wished to accept the condition of men in its totality. God, as the book of Genesis narrates, created man in a condition of immortality. In the terrestrial paradise he received only one prohibition: not to eat from the tree of the knowledge of good and evil. Obviously, in order to make us understand better, the biblical author uses metaphorical language: what is related is not understood in a literal sense. The message is received in the depth of its theological significance: for man, it is a trial of obedience and a recognition of the authority of God and of His lordship over creation. In order to make them deviate, the devil used two expedients with Adam and Eve, and he uses them also with us. Above all, he leads them to deny what God has imposed. For this the serpent says to Eve: "You will not die" (Gen. 3:4). He acts in the same way with us, when he makes us doubt the existence of sin and hell and paradise and of their eternity; or, for example, as in our times, where euthanasia and abortion are passed off as signs of humanity's progress. The second subterfuge is to make evil appear good, a gain rather than a loss. The serpent proceeds: "God knows that when you eat of it your eyes will be opened, and you will be like God, knowing good and evil" (Gen. 3:5). The devil also makes evil appear interesting, positive, and beautiful.

In light of this situation, by incarnating Himself, Jesus accepts the extreme consequences of this original sin, whose effect is death: "[I]n the day that you eat of it you shall die," warns God when placing man in Eden (Gen. 2:17). By incarnating Himself, the Son of Man has accepted—as man and only as man—the condition of mortality and all its limitations: hunger, thirst, fatigue, and sensibility to pain. He accepted—in order to save us—the extreme consequence, death, in order to defeat it with His Resurrection. This fact makes St. Paul cry out: "O death, where is thy victory? O death, where is thy sting?" (1 Cor. 15:55). Death has been defeated by Jesus! Included in the great consolation of eternal salvation—the Lord will dry each of our tears (cf. Rev. 21:4)—are those who are afflicted with spiritual evils. This is great news for our dear brothers and sisters who suffer so much.

The Consequences of Christ's Victory

Let us ponder what has just been said, lingering a bit on the mystery of the Passion, death, and Resurrection of the Lord. The last—the Resurrection—obtains three victories for us against the three condemnations imposed on Adam and Eve after the original sin. The first condemnation is death; the second regards our body, which falls into decay ("you are dust, and to dust you shall return" [Gen. 3:19]); the third is symbolized in the closing of the doors of paradise.

Above all, Jesus obtains victory over death; therefore, immediately after closing our eyes to this world, our body does not go into the semidarkness of Sheol; rather, it is destined to rise again. This plan is expressed very clearly in the affirmation Jesus expresses to the good thief on the cross: "Truly, I say to you, today you will be with me in Paradise" (Luke 23:43). This tells us that we must not fear death, because in death we are going toward the peace, harmony, and love that await us and give us life without end.

Here lies the victory over the second condemnation: man is made of soul and body and cannot live with the soul detached from the body. Body and soul are destined to reunite at the end of time, that is, at the moment of the Last Judgment. St. Thomas Aquinas—in my view, the greatest Christian theologian—affirms that, if in faith we believe in this unity between the soul and the body, even from a rational point of view (using only the power of reason), it is impossible to conceive them separated. If we think of the saints—who already enjoy paradise but whose bodies are still not united to their souls, since that will happen only at the end of time—we can be certain that they already live the beatified state without the body and that they will reach their highest level of blessedness when body and soul are rejoined. And through the mercy of God, the same can be said of us when we reach paradise. Only when time is completed, when the soul and the body are rejoined, will there be a true fullness of life. To say it in simple terms: for the moment, the saints have so much happiness that they can be content with only their souls. The same can be said inversely for the damned.

Finally, regarding the third condemnation, we can maintain that Jesus, by His Resurrection, has opened the doors of paradise for us, the doors that had been closed and sealed by original sin. This is the fundamental lesson of Easter, for which we can say with the joy of our faith that our life is destined to glory and eternal happiness, together with the company of Mary, the saints, and the most Holy Trinity.

Giving Meaning to Suffering

Yet we experience pain and suffering in this life. How do we look at eternal life for those who suffer in body and spirit? God created everything for love and happiness, but He also established that each creature arrive there freely and without constraint. The Lord has fixed a trial for everyone. The angels themselves were subjected to this test. We know the final result: some of them rebelled against God and did not wish to recognize His authority or to submit humbly to Him. These are the fallen who were definitively damned. The other angels preferred obedience to God, and they chose paradise.

Man is also subjected to the test of fidelity to God's laws. This happens in an eminent way during a time of suffering, which, as we well know, is experienced by everyone. "If any man would come after me, let him deny himself and take up his cross daily and follow me" (Luke 9:23). The Magisterium of the Church reminds us that "the messianic victory over sickness, as over all other human sufferings, does not happen only by its elimination through miraculous healing, but also through the voluntary and innocent suffering of Christ in his passion, which gives every person the ability to unite himself to the sufferings of the Lord."[4] Therefore, human suffering associated with Christ's becomes salvific: "In bringing about the Redemption through suffering, Christ *has also raised human suffering to the level of the Redemption.* Thus each man, in his suffering, can also become a sharer in the redemptive suffering of Christ."[5]

Pain, especially that of the innocent, is a mystery that overwhelms our capacity to understand. The sufferer, who bears the pain of illness or of some other spiritual evil, such as diabolical possession, is elevated to a level nearer to Christ, making him capable through faith of cultivating hope. Indeed, the sufferer is called to a true and proper vocation, that of participating in the increase of the Kingdom of God with new and more precious modalities. The words of the apostle Paul can become their model: "[I]n my flesh I complete what is lacking in Christ's afflictions for the sake

[4] Congregation for the Doctrine of the Faith, *Instruction on Prayers for Healing*, no. 1.

[5] St. John Paul II, apostolic letter *Salvifici Doloris* (On the Christian Meaning of Human Suffering), no. 19.

of his body, that is, the church" (Col. 1:24).[6] Offering oneself to the will of God in suffering is the only path one can take. It is the mystery that I encounter each day in my ministry of releasing so many brothers and sisters from the sufferings of evil spirits, sufferings that they, in turn, offer for the salvation of the world.

In order to translate these theological concepts into popular terms, let us borrow what was said in my region, in Emilia [Romagna]: "No one goes to heaven in a horse-drawn carriage." It's necessary somehow, to earn one's way. But let us understand that everything is grace; paradise can never be "merited." It is Christ alone who has earned it for everyone through the narrow passage of His Passion and death on the Cross that led to the joy of the Resurrection. We are given the opportunity to accept it through the trials of life. And this is so for everyone. We read, for example, that some saints endured extraordinary sufferings. But the Lord does not demand this from everyone. Each of us endures his tribulations, his ordinary and his extraordinary difficulties. To be tried in body and in spirit, entrusting oneself totally to God, is a true and proper test of faith, where love and fidelity to the Lord are given freely and not for some advantage. In brief, love for God has no other reason but love. Is it not also true of human love? Bernard of Clairvaux has illuminating words on the subject: "Love is sufficient of itself; it gives pleasure by itself and because of itself. It is its own merit, its own reward. Love looks for no cause outside itself, no effect beyond itself. Its profit lies in its practice; I love because I love."[7]

We are called, then, to love God and to believe in Him in the difficulties of life, because we recognize that the stormy things

[6] See *Instruction on Prayers for Healing*, no. 1.

[7] Cf. St. Bernard of Clairvaux, *Love of Bridegroom and Bride*, 83:4–6.

give us strength and the help to go forward each day. I cite again the example of St. Paul, who speaks of the "thorn in the flesh" (cf. 2 Cor. 12:7). We do not know exactly what he was suffering; he speaks of a "messenger of Satan" who was persecuting him. We can infer that it involved a physical suffering due to the action of the devil and not from natural causes. "Three times I besought the Lord about this, that it should leave me," he affirms, nearly desperate (2 Cor. 12:8). God, however, does not free him. "My grace is sufficient for you," He responds to him (2 Cor. 12:9), because virtue is manifested and deepened precisely through suffering, where virtue is tried and perfected. The apostle's experience confirms that we learn to love God through suffering, perfecting ourselves in love. Suffering—I repeat—offered as reparation for the salvation of souls and the conversion of sinners becomes an instrument of true collaboration with God's work for the redemption of all humanity.

The Signs of God's Love

How, then, is divine mercy manifested toward those who suffer and, in particular, toward those who are vexed by demons? The response is: through prayer, the intimate communion with Jesus, and in the highest way, in the sacraments, the tangible signs of God's love for us.

Those persons who experience spiritual disturbances suffer from a unique form of suffering: in the case of physical illnesses there are medical tests, and if doctors are able to understand the causes, they can make prognoses and often find suitable remedies at the right moment and proceed with the attempts. In the case of the sufferings caused by demons, no human or scientifically verifiable explanation exists. We are in the field of the invisible: no two cases are similar; each has its own story, and in each one it is very difficult, if not impossible, to know how things were developed. What is certain is that the interior suffering is always very great, and often not understood, at least at the beginning, not even by those who are around the afflicted person, such as relatives and friends. This situation often leads to great frustration and solitude in those who experience it. In the case of torments caused by demons, we find ourselves before a mystery that can be confronted solely through total abandonment to the will of God. It is indispensable to turn to Him, since no human cure exists other than the supernatural cure and the knowledge that comes from faith that one's life, even in paradoxical situations like these, "is hidden with Christ in God" (cf. Col. 3:3).

Thus, God's "prescriptions," authentic instruments of grace, become tangible signs that nurture faith and hope even when one confronts the most inexplicable situations. Many persons who suffer from spiritual maladies, and whom I have encountered over the years, confirm this each and every day.

2

Satan and the Fallen Angels

The Pride of Lucifer and His Acolytes

Let us now delve deeply into the topic of evil spirits—the identity of Satan and his followers, the demons—and let us proceed in an orderly manner. God, in His infinite power, created multitudes of angels, an impressive, incalculable number. Psalm 146 says that God knows the stars one by one and calls them by name. The same thing can be said of the angels: God knows them one by one. One day during an exorcism Father Candido Amantini—a Passionist priest and my great teacher[8]—asked a demon: "How many are you?" The demon responded: "We are so many that if we were visible we would obscure the sun." The demon on that occasion gave information that we have no reason to disbelieve because it is confirmed in the Bible.

God created the angels as extremely intelligent beings, with knowledge immensely superior to man's; and He predestined them to paradise, to eternal beatitude. Paradise, then, is not a passive and static contemplation of God. God Himself created

[8] Father Candido, whose cause for beatification was introduced on July 13, 2012, exercised the ministry of exorcism from 1961 to 1992 in Rome at the Church of the Holy Staircase (the staircase leading to the praetorium that Jesus ascended during His Passion).

everything in movement, both visible things—for example, the stars—and invisible things.

A great number of the angels fell because they rebelled against God. We recall that before admitting the angels to paradise, God subjected them to a trial of obedience and humility, of which we know the nature but not the specifics. The sin of the fallen angels was one of pride and disobedience. Satan, the most beautiful of all the angels, being aware of his extreme intelligence, rebelled at the idea of being subjected to someone. He forgot that he was a creature made by God. Many angels followed him in his folly of omnipotence and never turned back from their choice.

I note, incidentally, that this also happens with man, particularly in our day, when many appear to have forgotten God. The frenzy of omnipotence, of which men are often the victim in our times, seems to me precisely to reenter into this dramatic perspective of autonomy and complete self-referentiality.

Returning to our discourse: the original sins of the angels are the same as those who implicitly or explicitly adhere to Satanism. Angels and men who follow Satan base their existence on three principles and practical rules of life: you can do what you wish, that is, without subjugation to God's laws; you obey no one; and you are the god of yourself. We shall speak of this further on.

The Angels Who Chose God

Unlike the demons, the angelic creatures were humble, and therefore a choice opened up to them: the joyful and eternal Beatific Vision of God, the Creator. They chose to remain faithful to the nature and goal of their existence—that of praising God eternally—doing a simple and at the same time difficult thing: being humble and therefore free from pride. They accepted submission to God, that is, fidelity to their Creator and to His plan. In this way the angels fully embraced their nature and their end. It was a sign of faithfulness to the truth: they, like us, were created by God to love Him forever. This attitude does not humiliate them at all, because it does not imply a *lack* of something in any way; rather, to the contrary, a fullness. The angels have continued to be faithful to their nature, which refers them directly to God, the One who has written in creation the best laws for them, thought of for their own good.

Their sole activity is to praise God in eternity, obeying His every command. For this reason, I always exhort everyone, above all my particular clients, to invoke often their guardian angels, who protect us from dangers and who give us the proper suggestions at the right moments, even if they cannot impede us from being put under temptation and from eventually falling into sin.

What happened between the angels is narrated in the twelfth chapter of the book of Revelation: there was a great war between the angels who remained faithful to God and those who rebelled against Him — in brief, a war between the angels and the demons. In this passage, the Bible tells us that Michael the Archangel was at the head of the angels and that the dragon guided the angels who rebelled (and were defeated). The result was that "there was no longer any place for them in heaven" (Rev. 12:8). There also occurred something that Sacred Scripture does not mention, but that I personally have no motive to doubt: that the demons were free to create the inferno (hell), that is, to put themselves in a situation, in a state of life contrary to God, damning themselves eternally. With their choice they themselves gave form to their own environment.

Their new condition, recognized by the Bible as "infernal," implied that the devils were forever excluded from paradise, from the vision of God, and from eternal happiness, which originally was their only goal. Therefore, it is a truth of faith that the demons are definitively condemned, that is, damned: for them there is absolutely no possibility of salvation because their arrogant choice is unchangeable. Why? Because of their intelligence—which, in pure spirits, is greatly superior to ours—and because, unlike us men, they already enjoyed a full vision of God, they made their choice in a state of complete awareness, and it cannot be withdrawn. On the other hand, the demons would not wish to go back. The same can be said, but in the contrary, for the angels who chose God, and for the saints who have already merited the eternal vision of God, and for us who are called each day to respond to our call to sanctity.

Can the Devil Read Our Thoughts?

We have now arrived at the specific action of the devil, and we begin with the first question: Can the devil know our thoughts; is he able to understand what we are thinking at a certain moment in our life? The response is simple: absolutely not. Theology is agreed on this question. Only God—who is omniscient, who intimately possesses the secrets of created reality, that of men and angels, and that of uncreated reality, which is His own essence—knows in depth the thoughts of each man. Although a spiritual creature, the demon does not understand what is in our mind and in our heart; he can only surmise it through observing our behavior. It is not a complicated operation for him, having an extremely fine intelligence. If a young person smokes marijuana, for example, [the demon] can deduce that in the future he will also use stronger drugs. In a word: from what we read, see, say, and experience, and from the companions we choose, even from our glances—from all this he can discern where he will tempt us and at which particular moment. And that is what he does.

This brings to mind a passage from the first letter of St. Peter: "Brothers and sisters, be sober, be watchful. Your adversary the devil prowls around like a roaring lion, seeking some one to devour. Resist him, firm in your faith" (cf. 1 Pet. 5:8–9). My interpretation of this passage, on which various biblicists are agreed, sounds like this: "Brothers and sisters, be vigilant. The devil wanders around each one of you, searching where to devour." That word *where* is important: the devil looks in each person precisely for his weak point and "works" on it, creating his next sinful occasions, those that he has commissioned for him. It will be the targeted person himself, who in his liberty, will commit the sin, after having been well "cooked" by Satan's temptation.

The most frequent weak points in man are, from time to time, always the same: pride, money, and lust. And, let us note well, there are no age limits for sinning. When I hear confessions, I often say to my penitents, somewhat jokingly, that their temptations will end only five minutes after they have exhaled their last breath. Therefore, we must not presume or hope that at an advanced age we shall be exempt from sin. A vice that is cultivated in youth will not lessen in old age without some work and intervention. Let us consider lust: when I hear confessions, it's not uncommon for the elderly to confess to looking at pornography more often than the youth. The will to struggle against sin must be cultivated even to the end of our days.

Does the Devil Fear Man?

We proceed to the second question: Who must be afraid, us or the devil? The letter of James says textually: "Submit yourselves therefore to God. Resist the devil and he will flee from you" (James 4:7). The demon keeps his distance from the one who nurtures his faith, who frequents the sacraments, and who wishes to live devoutly. Why? Simply put, the devil hates God and is in terror of Him and anything that even has the odor of santicty. If we think about it, we can recall periods of our existence in which we have intensified our interior life and felt stronger in resisting temptations. On the other hand, we must avoid becoming arrogant and must always remember that the demon does not ever cease to tempt us, even to the end of our days.

I should also mention that sacred places, in particular those where a strong Marian devotion exists, have a similar effect. For these Satan has an invincible aversion: Loreto, Lourdes, Fátima, just to cite a few that are well known. Many liberations occur in these places.

I also wish to add that the devil can greatly disturb a person who nurtures his faith, but he does so unwillingly because he is "forced" to by the power of a spell. He prefers, far and away, to be involved with those who have distanced themselves from God. In these circumstances he is freer to act. Satan fears the sons of God, those seeking to conform their lives to Jesus: "I have been crucified with Christ; it is no longer I who live, but Christ who lives in me" (Gal. 2:20). The devil is aware that he is stronger and more intelligent than we are, but he also knows that we are not alone in the struggle against him. One example suffices: toward the sunset of his life, Don Bosco, one of the greatest saints of the nineteenth century, liberated a girl from possession simply by entering the chapel dressed in sacred vestments to celebrate Mass. The devil is in fear of the saints and their sanctity.

Often people will ask me if, during the process of liberation, the prayers denouncing Satan are useful. My response is: yes. Indeed, it is indispensable to recite them. Our liturgy also affirms it: the so-called renunciations of Satan and the questions on the articles of the Creed are purposely included in the rite of baptism, the sacrament with which we begin our Christian life. We also pronounce them during the Paschal Vigil, in confirmation of our faith. It is important to renounce Satan and all his works, but it is also important to recite the Creed often, as we say it at Mass on Sundays and on feast days. Moreover, the experiences of my ministry tell me that renouncing Satan and pronouncing the profession of our Faith are indispensable for those who have had some experience with the occult; it serves to break off every tie with the Evil One.

Where Does the Evil One Dwell in the Human Body?

Another recurring question is whether the demon is located in a specific part of the human body. The answer, without a doubt, is in the the negative. To put it as simply as possible, demons influence our body or one part of it without locating themselves in that particular organ or limb. When the possessed person falls into a trance and the Evil Spirit takes "control" in some way—inducing in him uncontrolled movements or making him speak or curse—it is as if the demon wraps around the entire body of the possessed, causing him to lose control of himself. Sometimes it can seem as if the spirit is localized in the throat, in the stomach, in the intestine, or in the head, where pains and spasms are manifested. In reality, the demon is not there in a specific part of the body but only influencing a specific organ within that moment.

If this is the way things are, do diabolical possessions and other spiritual evils exclude the presence of the Holy Spirit? We cannot reason in a human way with spirits. The represented space within the human body is not empty or refillable the way that a glass can be refilled by and emptied of water. In the case of the demon and the Holy Spirit, the two rival entities can live together—obviously in conflict—in the same person. On the other hand, we know that diverse saints were possessed by bad spirits, even if evidently they were filled with the Holy Spirit. How does one explain this if the demon does not occupy physical space? Certainly, the Holy Spirit can chase away the demon, but He does it within the boundaries of our own free will, thus permitting us to make our own choices. The Gospel of Mark says: "This kind [of demon] cannot be driven out by anything but prayer and fasting" (Mark 9:29). The demon always tries to minimize himself, to hide himself, because he knows that as soon as his presence is obvious to the outside world, it could be the beginning of his end. The person would then begin to pray more intensely, to submit to exorcisms and prayers of deliverance, to intensify his participation at the Mass, et cetera. Beyond a certain limit, the devil is not able to resist the power of prayer and fasting. Obviously, this is not always the case, so it probably occurs through a mysterious divine permission, or through the exceptional efficacy of the completed rite. But more often the demon is deeply ingrained and difficult to uproot, and exorcisms may continue for years and years.

Who ought to pray and fast? Everyone—the person struck by the spiritual evil and those close to him. For the first, it is a trial of extraordinary faith, a response to a very particular call to sanctity. For the others, it is an appeal to demonstrate Christian charity concretely. Indeed, the prayers of close family members are very efficacious; their collaboration can be very helpful in creating a positive climate in the house. To these persons I add the exorcist, the pastor, friends, and whoever lends a hand in the liberation of the obsessed.

What Does the Devil Look Like?

Among the most recurring questions, and in my opinion the most amusing, is: How does the devil appear or what does he look like? He is a pure spirit; he does not have corporeal substance; therefore, he is not representative to us in a fully comprehensible form. It is the same for him as for the angels: if they wish to appear to men, they must assume characteristics accessible to us. The Bible is filled with visions of angels as men. In the book of Tobias, for example, the Archangel Raphael accompanies the young Tobias on his mission by assuming the form of a youth. In the Gospels, we find it particularly worth noting the form of the Archangel Gabriel at the Annunciation to Mary (Luke 1:26–38).

Returning to the appearance of the devil: one can say that, in his essence, he is much uglier than we can even vaguely imagine. His horrific appearance is a direct consequence of his distancing himself from God and of his explicit and irrevocable choice of rebellion. This we can infer from logical reasoning: if God is infinitely beautiful, whoever decides to distance himself [from God] must be the exact opposite. Naturally, this is only one type of theological augmentation that we find based on revelation and from the support of our natural reason when it is illuminated by faith.

And if, stretching the discourse, we wished somehow to give the demon an image? We begin, necessarily, by setting aside the figures derived from traditional depictions of the devil with horns, a tail, the wings of a bat, talons, and inflamed eyes. Being a pure spirit, evidently he cannot embody these characteristics. If these images can help us to fear his actions toward us — and we have good reason to — then we should welcome them; on the other hand, we risk making the devil appear like an ancient relic, a frill of times past, and the stuff of simpletons. There is a great danger in over-relying on these images, and they can be of service to the devil! It is necessary to say that certainly, in his decadent liberty, he can appear to men and women through the semblances of a monstrous animal or as a person with Mephistophelian (satanic) characteristics. Some of the hair-raising designs printed on the T-shirts worn by young people that we see everywhere give me cause for concern; and I advise them to get rid of them. But the devil, being very shrewd, can also assume innocuous forms. The case of St. Pio of Pietrelcina is exemplary. At times, the devil showed himself to him as a ferocious dog, at other times as Jesus or as our Lady, at still other times as his confessor or as the father guardian of his convent, who commanded him to do something. But after verifying the order he received with his superior, he understood that he had had a vision of the devil. There were even a few times when the devil appeared as a beautiful, naked girl.

Finally the demon could present himself with unpleasant odors, such as sulfur or animal excrement (it happens at times when one is blessing a house), or, to persons particularly sensitive, with odious noises, such as a clearly perceived rustling of the wind, or harassing tactile sensations.

What Does the Church Say of Wandering Souls?

Let us now confront another topic. Someone attests to seeing and perceiving "spirits." Are they only imaginings? Does it involve "wandering souls"? Regarding this we must be very prudent and discerning. The "presences," spirits or ghosts, are seen in particular literature and in the vast exorcistical caseload. There are persons, for example, who affirm perceiving the closeness, at times even physical, of ancestors or of unknown persons, "wandering souls," discerned as souls of the deceased that have not yet found their placement in the order of eternal life. At times there appear guides made up of spirits or souls that council persons on the most judicious decisions to take. What can be said [about these things]?

There are, above all, the certitudes of our Faith. The first is that we have only one life, and we play it out here; at the end, we shall be judged to be worthy to rise to life in God or to be unworthy, distancing ourselves from Him eternally. Therefore, there is not any possibility that these "wandering souls" are waiting to be incarnated, as maintained by some trends of spiritism. It is an idea that is absolutely incompatible with revelation and with faith in the resurrection of the flesh.

The second [certitude of our Faith] is that a form of communication exists between the dead and us: it is the principle of the Mystical Body, of the Church that communicates to her interiority, to her inner self. Specifically, there is a spiritual exchange between the souls of the dead in paradise and in purgatory and those of us still on our earthly pilgrimage that is manifested through the prayers of intercession. In particular, the souls in purgatory who are experiencing purification have the capacity to offer their suffering in extraordinary reparation for us; they, in turn, greatly enjoy the benefits of our prayers. Excluded are the souls of the damned; being in hell they do not enjoy (and do not desire) our prayers.

Returning to the wandering spirits: in my view, if immediately after death we go to paradise, to hell, or to purgatory, it is doubtful that wandering souls exist. In the old ritual of exorcism, one was put on guard against "presumed" possessions or spiritual disturbances caused by the damned soul of a deceased. It is, instead, the devil who is disguised like this. It happened to me, for example, that during an exorcism a spirit claimed to be one of these wandering spirits. A deeper verification revealed that he was a demon. But other exorcists are convinced of the contrary: according to them, the presence of such wandering spirits is a fact. Therefore, we shall speak of it again when we cover spiritism in chapter 4. Since it concerns a problem that is still unresolved, theologians will have to study it deeply through Scripture, the Magisterium of the Church, and the experience of mystics and seers.

3

The Cult of Satan and Its Manifestations

Occultism

The *Encyclopedia Treccani* defines *occultism* as a "set of doctrines founded on a religious, metaphysical, and physical concept of the universe that presupposes the existence of an array of dynamic forces—personal and impersonal, physical or psychic—that are not accessible with the instruments of logic or of the mathematical and experimental sciences [from this point of view they remain occult, that is, hidden or concealed], but with which a few of the learned are able to establish relationships through cognitive instruments or technical practices." Occultism is, in other words, the great umbrella under which all the practices and forms of satanic adoration are gathered in order to be drawn upon by those who wish to profit from its gains.

The most significant forms of occultism are magic, astrology, fortune-telling, and or spiritism. At its base is the belief in the existence of spiritual forces that cannot be experienced through one's external senses (i.e., touch, sight, and so forth); therefore, they are esoteric or hidden. By controlling these forces through techniques into which one is initiated (and which parallel the techniques of esoterism) and after practicing them appropriately, one can dominate the reality. These entities, as we shall see, are the unclean spirits commonly called devils. The reality is more complex, however, because the occultists, in order to enjoy their powers, end with putting themselves at the service of the superior hierarchies: after all, the leader of the sects into which they enter is Satan himself, who asks a very high price of those he serves.

Satanism

Satanism is the practice of the cult, or worship, of Satan. It is necessary to say that Satanists and Satanism truly exist; they are not simply in the mind of some imaginative Hollywood director. To be precise, a Satanist is one who explicitly decides to consecrate himself—that is, to give himself, through a ritual—to Satan and to enter into a sect. These cases are fairly rare: we are speaking of thousands, not millions of persons. Although they are few, they are extremely dangerous to souls. These people, who are leading a life of sin, are exclusively orientated toward themselves, and they follow the teachings of the Prince of Darkness to the letter.

Generally one distinguishes [between] a personal Satanism (or occultism) and an impersonal or rationalist Satanism. The first recognizes the personal nature of Satan, and the followers entreat, adore, and honor him as a god. The second, the impersonal or rationalist, does not believe in Satan's personal nature, that is, in the metaphysical sense; rather, they see him as a cosmic energy that is present in each man and in the world and that, when called upon, will emerge in all his power to carry out the most absurd and atrocious perversions, always connecting them to esoteric rites.

What is their objective? Satanists wish to develop this depraved form of devotion through a diffusion of the theory and practice of three basic principles: you can do all that you wish, no one has the right to command you, and you are the god of yourself. The first principle intends to confer full liberty to the adherent on everything he wishes to do, without limits. The second is the release from the principle of authority, that is, from any obligation to obey parents, the Church, the state, and whoever places restrictions in the name of the common good. The third denies all the truth that comes directly from God: paradise, the inferno, purgatory, judgment, the Ten Commandments, the precepts of the Church, Mary, and so forth.

In appearance these principles are seductive, especially for younger people, because they delude them into thinking that life is a beautiful holiday in an imaginary land of playthings, where everything is permitted and where your "I" does not recognize any limits regarding pleasure and enjoyment. It is my conviction as well as my heartfelt advice to all parents that—in order to help their children disdain this perspective with its destructive nature—it is necessary to educate them from an early age to cultivate a life of faith through prayer, through the Mass, and through association with the various Catholic youth clubs and other similar organizations. It is absolutely necessary to give them a sense of God and the awareness of the existence of sin and the Devil, the tempter who wishes to lead us to a separation from God and therefore to death. These young people, then, when they become older, will probably have developed the right attitudes toward these sects and satanic practices. I am aware that it involves a difficult form of education, but let us always remember that, because of the total absence of beautiful and good ideals, young people today are more exposed to these dangers. When faith disappears, one abandons himself to superstition and occultism.

Let us return to the Satanists. Since baptized Christians are commonly called children of God, can Satanists be called children of Satan? For them, this is not conceivable. Satan does not desire brothers or friends, much less children. Satan desires only slaves, whom he buys by promising them a guaranteed and unlimited enjoyment of things with—and here is the great lie—unchecked liberty, which is the foundation of Satanism itself.

Consecration to Satan

How does one become a Satanist? Through a rite of consecration to Satan, the person hands himself over to Satan in body and soul, asks to be received among his hosts, and thus enters into a sect. It normally involves an agreement written in blood, which sounds more or less like this: "Satan, from now on I belong to you, in life, in death, and after death. Accept me as your acolyte. I give you my body and my soul, and I shall do what you wish and command, but give me pleasures, success, sex, and riches." Usually the consecration happens during a collective rite, often with a black mass, in which one is initiated into the sect and into the satanic practices.

The contract of blood can also be done individually, as with religious vows, which can be made publicly, before an assembly of the people of God—usually during a communal celebration—or privately and singularly in secret before God.

All these cases concern a true and proper selling of the soul to the devil, who maintains his tragic promises, but without ever giving any happiness but only innumerable sufferings. In a word, being consecrated to the devil guarantees a life of pure hell on earth and an eternal hell in the afterlife. In my experience, these persons do not ever receive peace, and they leave behind them a trail of sorrow, solitude, and death.

The spread of Satanism does not occur solely one on one. Many books and pamphlets circulate among young people, and there are also Internet sites that teach the formulas of consecration to the Prince of Darkness. It is an extremely dangerous practice. It may be done as a joke or seriously, alone or in a group—it makes no difference, because it can bear very heavy consequences, even years later, when after having settled down with a spouse, children, and a good job, one must still confront a burdensome diabolical possession. For this reason it is necessary to think of the consequences of such a choice, which is often irreversible or at least very difficult to reverse. I know persons who have left, but only after an enormous struggle, and often while being threatened by the followers. Even more, they always remain marked in their psyche and in their body, often enduring years and years of exorcisms in order to be liberated from the devil and the diabolical possessions on their backs. In brief, it is not a great business.

In recent times, various cases of sensational homicides have been reported in the media that are surely ascribable to a particular influence of Satan, perhaps the result of some pact contracted with him. For example, there is the case of the three girls of Chiavenna who in June of 2000 killed Sister Maria Laura Mainetti. From what I read, I do not believe that they were possessed by demons; rather, I believe that they acted under Satan's potent inspiration: the cynicism, the brutality, the lack of restraint in the wounding of that poor religious could not have been solely their own invention. Immediately afterward, two of the three went to an amusement park, while the third went home to clean the kitchen knife they used to kill her, replacing it in the drawer. This incredible story confirms the risks that are in play for today's young people.

Today in Italy there are a few hundred satanic sects; generally each one has a few members. It is difficult to do a precise charting of them, because they always act in the shadows.

I wish to conclude with an important observation. It is not necessary to become a Satanist in order to serve the devil and become one of his followers. There are many, alas, who do not officially consecrate themselves to Satan but choose to follow his basic principles, and as a result they place their souls at great risk.

The Powers That Come from Satan

One might wonder what powers the devil gives to his devotees—along with the indecipherable sufferings. There is an interminable list. Some powers are clearly of a diabolical origin; others require some discernment.

Typical powers that are the direct consequence of the sale of one's soul to the devil and of the Satanist's adopted identity at consecration: riches, free sex, and unlimited power. At the beginning everything comes easily and seems to be a great and beautiful affair. But all of it involves false illusions: not long afterward, indescribable sufferings take over, signs that the devil has "taken them for a ride," because his objective is to make you a slave and ruin your life.

I related a testimony of this dramatic reality in a book, *The Last Exorcist* (the case of Simona) written with the journalist Paolo Rodari.[9] This young woman had accepted the offer of consecrating herself to Satan in exchange for a luminous career. Soon afterward, she scaled the heights of her company, earning an impressive salary and a high social reputation: the devil had maintained his promise. But in exchange he truly asked for her soul: she found herself living with intense mo-

[9] Cf. Gabriele Amorth and Paolo Rodari, *L'ultimo esorcista* (Milan: Piemme, 2012).

ments of hatred toward certain individuals that were so strong and sudden that each time she would have to shut herself in the bathroom, beating her fists and her head against the wall and screaming with pain. She bitterly repented it, and only after a long journey, which I made with her, did she manage to regain her liberty definitively; but the price was high; she had to give back the "gifts" given to her by Satan; and even before she had a chance to renounce her career, she was fired; but this time she was completely free.

These powers that the spiritists call "gifts" can also be tied to magic rites (spells, the evil eye, charms, et cetera) done personally or under submission. Among these, which I cite only as examples are: foresight (the capacity to see things that will happen in the future), clairvoyance (the possibility of seeing things and persons in other places that are not visible), visions and apparitions, the phenomena of automatic writing (the inspiration to write messages dictated by external entities), levitation, bilocation, and poltergeist activity (the sudden and unexplainable movement of objects). At other times they can hear "voices" that suggest prayer or curses, or have visions, or even feel lightly touched by a spiritual entity. Some of these phenomena can be attributed to the supernatural—that is, to God—but only when there is convincing proof; otherwise, when they are suspicious enough, I tend to place them in the sphere of the preternatural—that is, the diabolical. But it is always the Church that must determine their divine provenance.

What I recommend first in these cases is not to pay attention to these voices, visions, and interior inspirations and to refuse these powers expressively, always calling on the Virgin Mary for spiritual help. I also advise a person to place himself in the hands of a spiritual adviser, a priest, who will ponder the matter. In the case of the persistence of the phenomena, one can ask to receive some exorcisms and some prayers of deliverance in order to verify that these powers are not associated, as it often happens, with an evil spell: possession, vexation, obsession, and infestation. Never, and I say never, should one feel privileged and therefore inspired to use these powers: it would be like saying yes to Satan.

The Black Mass: A Parody of the Eucharistic Celebration

I have spoken of the black mass as a ceremony during which the consecration to Satan occurs. The black mass is a parody of [the Catholic] Mass, in which one adores and exalts Satan. Usually it is officiated at night, because the darkness permits greater secrecy and because during the night fewer people are found at prayer, which disturbs the ritual.

During the celebration, the words and the external signs of the Eucharistic liturgy are used, but always in a contrary sense, in order to manifest opposition to God. There is always a satanic priest officiating who wears blasphemous vestments, an altar represented by a nude woman, possibly a virgin, on whom very serious acts of profanity of the Eucharist (usually stolen from a church), are performed, with words of consecration proclaimed in a contrary sense and an overturned crucifix. Only members of the satanic sect, who are sworn to secrecy, may participate. Nonmembers are never permitted to attend unless it is hoped that, having already been seduced by the perversions and the illusion of power, they may decide to enter the sect. In general the black masses are celebrated by small groups of ten or at most fifteen of the "faithful."

Once the ritual is concluded, the woman who functions as the altar is raped in turn by all the participants: first by the one who exercised the "rites" of the priest, then by all the others. This woman may have freely accepted that role, or she may have been led there against her will; and aside from the physical violence, she often suffers the terrible consequences of the ritual: [diabolical] possession.

As in the Church, some of the official rites are required and are tied to particular feast days. The most important is Halloween, which falls on the night between October 31 and November 1 of each year: it is considered the magic New Year. Therefore, it is necessary to understand the extreme danger for our children and youth who participate in the feast of Halloween on that date. The second precedes our feast of the presentation of Jesus in the Temple on February 2. The night before, in fact, begins the magic spring. The summer magic is the third satanic "solemnity" and occurs on the night between April 30 and May 1. During the year [Satanists] often choose nights when the new moon is inaugurated, because it is particularly dark.

The officiator of these rites is usually someone who is consecrated to Satan, and although it is not stated, this person is also usually possessed by the devil. It may also not be so. I am certain, however, that during these rituals, as stated above, the Eucharistic hosts are profaned, [having been] stolen from tabernacles or taken by some of the faithful at Communion during Mass and not consumed.

I once exorcised a person who had purloined a consecrated Host during a Mass in order to participate at a black mass. He robbed Hosts everywhere, even though he had already begun a courageous path toward liberation. According to what he told me, he was acting in a state of complete unconsciousness—that is, in the state of a trance typical of persons possessed by the devil.

Black Magic: A Grave Sin against the Faith

We now arrive at the central point of our discourse: magic. It would not have made sense to speak of Satanism and black masses without seriously confronting the subject of magic. On this topic the *Catechism of the Catholic Church* furnishes the best definition: "All practices of *magic* or *sorcery*, by which one attempts to tame occult powers, so as to place them at one's service and have a supernatural power over others—even if this were for the sake of restoring their health—are gravely contrary to the virtue of religion" (no. 2117). The Church condemns such practices on the basis of revelation and on the conviction that in spiritism and occultism it is the devil who is acting. The exorcists, as always, testify to this without a shadow of a doubt.

The definition of magic tells us two things. Above all, it has ambition—through the utilization of evil spells, the evil eye, charms, magic filters, rituals, invocations, cursed foods and drinks ingested by the victims, crystal balls, et cetera—to modify and foretell the course of human events, and to utilize the preternatural (demoniac) powers to make a person fall in love, be cured of an illness, be dismissed from a job, kill someone, provoke atmospheric events, et cetera. In other words, magic is a practice used to do evil things and to influence people and the reality created by the devil. This is also valid for the rites that are commonly called "white magic" and that are done for the "good"—in the sense that they promote ends that are not apparently wicked, as, for example, finding a job—and "red magic," which regards the sphere of sexuality and influences the sentiments. All turn to the same preternatural entity, the wizard, who, in all these cases, resorts to the power of Satan in order to obtain the invoked result. Therefore, there is no difference among them, "black," "white," or "red." It is enough to see the effects of all of them. I personally knew the case of a girl who was turning to a wizard in order to make the young man she was in love with leave his fiancée so that she could marry him. Alas, the thing worked; first, the young man left his fiancée, and then he married the girl who had commissioned the spell: the marriage was a real Calvary.

The second aspect that emerges from the *Catechism*'s definition is that magic is seriously contrary to the First Commandment: "You shall have no other gods before me" (Exod. 20:3). Whoever turns to witches, fortune-tellers, occultists, or wizards, commits a very serious sin of superstition, which is contrary to faith. But what is superstition? The term *superstition* derives from the Latin *superstitio* and indicates when something is superimposed on another, distorting the original sense. One is superstitious when one believes that something innocent in itself brings misfortune (the classic black cat that crosses one's path, spilling salt on the pavement, breaking a mirror) or that it brings luck (the rabbit's foot, an iron horseshoe, crossing one's fingers)—that is, when one attributes to certain objects or deeds a power based on their intrinsic essence.

There are superstitions that also regard religious deeds or facts, such as superimposing a true piety on a false religion, that is, attributing power to objects and rites that are exteriorly Christian. This happens when practices and rites are carried out or formulas of our Faith are professed, making all their efficacy depend on rigid observances or preestablished forms and times: for example, on November 2, a certain number of souls will be freed from purgatory. Here it is evident that a magical mentality is present that deforms the true piety. In the case cited, it is only the mercy of God that can freely deliver a certain number of souls from purgatory. Our intercession, which is always appropriate, would be thwarted by this mentality that demands using prayer as a secret technique to obtain results, nearly "forcing" God to grant them. True piety in prayerful supplication places everything in God's hands, knowing that He, in His liberty and sovereignty, whether pleasing us or not, will always act for our good and for the persons and situations for which we pray.

This mixing of the sacred and the profane, which unfortunately is so present today even in the Christian community—for example, the hanging of a horseshoe around a statue of the Madonna in order to implore good luck—is superstitious. It leads individuals to divination, magic, and witchcraft, with the expectation of gaining supernatural power over their neighbors. As the *Catechism* says, "even if this were for the sake of restoring their health," it is "gravely contrary to the virtue of religion."

Unfortunately, there are many who resort to witches or wizards. Our own Western world, rich and hypertechnological, has much in common with primitive populations and with the culture of the late Middle Ages; both knew the preternatural powers well. Even today many persons still wink at magic and its priests, wizards, and sorcerers. One of my dear friends, a scholar, who died in 2005, Cecilia Gatto Trocchi, claimed that in Italy there were more than 13 million Italians who patronized sorcerers—a tsunami compared with the paltry number of priests and exorcists in the country! The only remedy—even if the episode occurred many years ago—is to issue an invitation to all those involved to repent and to confess this sin, with the firm intention of not doing anything so foolish again.

At this point, a question comes to mind: Is a person in God's grace preserved from the effects of magical rites? It is certainly more difficult to strike a person in such a state, although it is not impossible; being that each thing is freely at God's disposition, an evil can be permitted to be transmitted through a magical act and to do damage to one who lives in communion with God.

The Most Common Examples of Magic Are Evil Spells

"Evil spells" is a generic phrase, which includes all the forms in which someone is harmed through the occult (hidden) action of the devil and its various rites. Among those they make use of are spells, the evil eye, curses, macumba, voodoo, and satanic rites, to cite the most common. The objectives are to divide, to kill, to make fall in love, to make ill, to destroy, to lead to suicide, and to divide spouses, the engaged, and friends.

In order to bring about an evil spell, three things are necessary: a witch or a wizard, a person who commissions the witch or wizard, and an object on which the ritual is performed. As the sacraments have visible signs—for example, bread and wine in the Eucharist—evil spells also have theirs—such as clothing, photos, personal items, and foods—that are cursed by the wizard with formulas and rituals that are intended to produce negative spiritual effects on the persons affected. The sacraments, which work *ex opere operato* (from the work performed), do not confer grace without the personal dispositions of faith and acceptance on the part of the faithful who are enjoying them. Magic functions differently: the wizard must "win over" the action of the evil spirit, pressing it into service with invocations and prayers. The effect on the victim, however, is separate from his own personal inclinations, although, as I have said, a person in a state of grace with God is less vulnerable to the attack of an evil spell.

How Evil Spells Can Manifest Themselves

Some years ago, I exorcized a young man who had broken up with his fiancée after a six-year engagement. Soon after, he began to complain of sudden physical disturbances. Added to that fact was the impossibility, verified during a long period, of finding another fiancée or a job. It was then discovered during the prayer of the exorcism that the aspiring mother-in-law was not resigned to the breakup of her daughter's engagement and had commissioned an evil spell from a witch. The young man turned to me, and, after some exorcisms, the physical ills nearly disappeared, even if he was not able to find another fiancé or another job.

Another case is that of a man who opened a shop in a city plaza. The business was doing well. Then one day a competitor opened a business in that same plaza. Suddenly no one, not even the most loyal clients, would set foot in the first shop. In that case I verified a sort of local infestation: thus I celebrated some Masses inside the shop and personally imparted blessings and local exorcisms. Slowly the clients returned. How did I become aware that something was not right? The complete and sudden change was too suspicious to be normal. In this type of case, where reasonable social or scientific explanations are lacking, it is always appropriate to do something, a fine benediction, for example.

The evil eye is a different case, rarer and even less easy to figure out: it involves tossing out a spell through the power of a glance, with the objective of "sending over" the devil. It has nothing to do with popular traditions, such as carrying a good-luck charm or looking crosseyed at someone. Rather, it involves a true and proper rite. I must say, however, that I have never had a case clearly tied to this practice.

Is a person ever aware of having suddenly been subjected to a spell? It is difficult, although theoretically possible, that a person who has been subjected to an evil spell may never in the course of his life be aware of it. Above all, it is necessary to say that spells do not always reach their targets, either because the person may be well protected in his life of grace, or because God may not permit it, or because the wizard or sorcerer may not succeed, perhaps because the demon, the Prince of Lies, can deceive his own followers.

At other times, they hit the mark (and we shall treat the results in the next chapter when we speak of individual evil spirits, diabolical possession, physical and psychological obsessions, and local infestations). This can happen also at a distance of much time. Here are some examples. I have had cases involving persons who did not know that they had been subjected to spells until they were casual participants in a prayer-of-liberation service with a group of the Catholic Charismatic Renewal. In that circumstance they suddenly began to feel sick, to shout, and to curse, which for them was absurd and unthinkable behavior. After they discovered the evil spell, they immediately began to repair the situation by beginning a serious journey of faith — which is always necessary in these cases — by participating in a prayer encounter, and subjecting themselves to exorcisms.

Another interesting question is when does the evil spell occur? There are countless responses. For instance, it can occur in the womb, even before the victim's birth. It can also occur during infancy or in youth or adolescence. I recall a spell in which a little girl was told, "You will never marry." She was a beautiful girl, good and smart. When she grew up, all her engagements were inevitably broken off for the oddest reasons. Another cursed person whom I followed for a long time was left by his future spouse on the day of the wedding. Everything was ready: home, church, rings, invitations, restaurant ... Then, on the fated day, she did not present herself. A spell had been cast against that spousal union. At other times, the rites are completed later, at a more mature age or during the victim's old age.

It is necessary to remember that a spell can also activate itself—through the will of the wizard or the client—at some time in the future, such as at the moment of baptism or a marriage. In that case, the disturbance—often the diabolical possession—is "scheduled" to begin on that particular day. In the case of the baptism of a baby, it is difficult to establish it with certainty since the infant is not able to describe the disturbances he has suffered; generally the parents understand it sometime in the future, when the child is able to describe his ailments.

It is always important to understand the circumstances, the time, and the place of the evil's initiation as well as the persons who commission the spell. At times, it involves a relationship, even a very old one, that is characterized by perfidy, hate, and antipathy toward the victim. It is also necessary to know that spells are often inflicted through the preparation of foods to be ingested by the victims. Obviously it is very difficult to prevent this type of spiritual poisoning.

I am often asked if the wizards or the witches themselves, those who cast the spells, are always necessarily possessed? I think so, even if they are not aware of it or do not believe in these things. Magicians, wizards, sorcerers, and witches know that they have certain powers—it is something that gives them immense pleasure—and they use them to make people suffer, which also gives them pleasure. Furthermore, the wizards themselves will often submit to the spells, naturally for profit, since they do everything for money. Then the practice of magic worsens their situation.

Prayer can counter evil spells, and if done with faith and love, it reaches its objective, which is the heart of God. We also know that God Himself will dispose of things according to a plan whose ultimate end is always a greater good: eternal life. Each prayer prayed with this intention is effective. And at times, the Lord, in His infinite goodness, will grant us assistance and graces that are much greater than the fruit of our prayer.

Wizards, Fortune-Tellers, and Witches

One cannot speak of magic without speaking of wizards or sorcerers, those who are particularly adept at attracting and influencing the unfortunates who turn to them in a state of prostration over a personal matter or for the other superstitious attitudes already mentioned. They receive their clients in a study purposely decked out with small statues of our Lady, the saints, candles, incense, soft light, and everything that serves to create a magical, esoterical atmosphere, so useful in subjugating the naive adventurers.

No one doubts that there are many braggarts, false charismatics, and false wizards in circulation. They may even be the majority. They advertise on television, in magazines, and today, above all, on the Internet. They are swindlers who make money at the expense of the poor simpletons who entrust themselves to them to resolve their problems. The false wizards complete their rites without obtaining any evident result. For example, they give a charm or an amulet (at a high price obviously) in order to protect the client from something, or they hand him a sack filled with dirt taken from a cemetery and flavored with the bones of the dead and menstrual blood—and all without resolving anything. Above all, in order keep a hold on the client, they make him return each month to "recharge" and to pour out more change.

On the other hand, there are true wizards and witches who are often disguised as "seers" who practice occultism, spiritism, and Satanism as a true and proper profession. Perhaps they are a minority, but they are extremely effective. Through their rituals and the action of Satan, these people truly obtain what they seek—that is, the misery of their unfortunate victims through sickness, the loss of a job, the breakup of relationships or forced marriages or engagements, the collapse of business affairs, and physical and psychological illnesses. The history of cases is infinite. What is certain is that they turn to the occult forces, seeking their services. They are the idolaters and the worshippers of false gods who consistently try to gain some personal advantage. They are apostates because they favor the action of the devil, who, although he has already been defeated by the Resurrection of Christ and its effects in the Church, is still operative in the world, thanks also to their perfidy.

The dramatic increase in the number of possessed persons and spiritual disturbances makes me say that the malice and superstition of those who resort to them—including those who, even as a joke, practice forms of occultism, such as séances—has grown in correspondence with the generalized decline of the Faith and the spreading of a culture favoring magic. Television series such as *Witches* and films such as *Harry Potter* are in my view a devastating means of sowing suspicion in the minds of young people (and the not so young) and of cultivating a magical mentality. What is a magical mentality, if not thinking that reality can be modified with the wave of a wand?

Also relevant to the topic is how one becomes a wizard. There is a type of bona fide initiation, along with courses that introduce a person to this "art." One does not learn in the blink of an eye how to recite formulas, perform rituals, or use instruments of healing or prediction, such as pendulums, palm reading, divining, and fortune-telling cards. I believe that the paths of initiation are very diverse because they involve occultists, who do not wish to operate in the light of day. There is also the *Book of Commands*, a very ancient text of black magic that is accessible to those who are entrusted with the transmission of its very powerful formulas.

Wizards work mostly at night. After appeasing Satan with some "appropriate" rites of adoration, they act on photographs, puppets, or other objects belonging to the one who will be struck; then, through the intervention of the spirits the wizards invoke, the spiritually negative effects ritually propitiated on such objects will be transferred to the person himself.

It is necessary to clarify that all the consequences of the occult—possessions, obsessions, the evil eye, strange powers, and similar things—having been caused by the influence of Satan and activated by wizards, cannot, evidently, be reversed by them. On the contrary, their intervention would only worsen things. At times they boast of being exorcists, but what they claim as powers of liberation from evil spells are nothing but a product of Satan. In the end, one is always worse than before, and with the additional weight of a personal tie to a wizard. It is necessary to distrust a wizard who boasts of such powers. A demon is not chased away with a demon, only with prayer. In these cases it is necessary to resort to a priest, an exorcist, or the prayer groups of the Catholic Charismatic Renewal.

Finally, I am often asked if wizards can go back to the Faith. Wizards—like exorcists, even if obviously on the completely opposite side—touch the invisible world with their hands. When a true wizard sells himself to Satan, his reasoning is no longer his own, and normally he does not have the strength to liberate himself. For this reason, I believe that it is difficult, if not impossible, to convert back to God. God will seek to redeem him, even to the end, as He does with all His children. An exorcist related to me the case of a witch who remained in agony on her deathbed for many hours and who, amid great pains and sufferings, was unable to die. By chance, the exorcist had found himself at the hospital where the witch was languishing and did an exorcism on her, and after a while she expired—reconciled with God, we hope.

Spiritism

Spiritism is the evocation of the dead through a medium.[10] The medium is a type of spiritist priest who functions as a channel or means of communication with the spiritual world, in order to learn hidden things or to know the fate of a dearly departed. There are, in fact, many—unilluminated by Christian faith—who, at the death of a dear person or in the unrestrained desire to know the future, turn, out of desperation, to mediums, often with inauspicious effects on their lives.

How does the evocation of the dead occur? It happens through various techniques that come from a very ancient tradition—which, like those involved in other types of magic—have been developed and perfected by spiritist movements that have studied and practiced them in depth since the second half of

[10] Spiritism, or necromancy (from the Greek *necrós*, "dead," and *manzia*, "divination"), is a common practice in traditional cultures, particularly African and South American, and very diffuse in the West since the latter half of the 1800s.

the 1800s. Since then, spiritism has evolved into a universal religion that, guided by spirits, is expected [by its followers] to overcome the traditional religions and draw all humanity to a new era of brotherhood.[11] Culturally and politically, it resembles Freemasonry, to which many members of spiritism belong. Their techniques are easily accessed, and for this reason they constitute an easy entrance for the curious who wish to venture in. The most common is the séance, in which several persons are seated around a table, holding hands or resting them on the surface, with little fingers touching in order to maintain physical contact, as through a chain. If the evocation of the spirit succeeds, the table moves itself and "speaks" by striking some blows, which have a conventional meaning (for example one blow for yes, and two for no). The evoked spirit can also speak through the medium, who, having fallen into a trance, "lends" his voice to the spirit, or through a pendulum, through automatic writing (in which, always during the trance, the medium writes what he says is dictated by the spirit), or through a Ouija board, on which a little plate or a coin is moved, going from one letter of the alphabet to another to form words and concepts that the spirits wish to reveal.

Also here, as in magic, there are many braggarts who look to make money at the expense of those who are suffering. But there are also many mediums who are truly able to get in contact with spiritual entities. These presumed spirits of the dead often reveal things that are unknown to the medium himself but are known to

[11] This is diffusely discussed by François-Marie Dermine in his book *Carismatici, sensitive e medium: Il confine della mentalitá magica* (Bologna: ESD, 2010), 56ff. The text constitutes an excellent basis from which to deepen the theme of spiritism and, in general, the paranormal phenomena, including Christian.

the client, who, once conquered by the credibility of the "voice," does not hesitate to believe all the other revelations in future sessions. Often these voices announce beautiful things or leave edifying messages that are difficult to ignore. In brief, spiritism in these cases seems to work, and it draws many followers.

The fact, then, that they are able to obtain information about events that have truly happened and are unknown to the medium leads us to attribute these communications to an intelligent external cause—that is, to spirits. But of what exactly are we speaking? According to an important trend in spiritism, that of Allan Kardec,[12] they are souls in the temporal stage between one reincarnation and another that are in sight of their progressive elevation and are wandering: being disincarnated, they are, therefore, available to speak. Good spirits are distinguished from spirits that are less good, depending on their level of perfection. All of this, of course, is completely contrary to Christian doctrine. There are no good spirits other than angels and no bad spirits other than demons.

Another, more ethnic trend, like that of the traditional Afro-American cults, holds that these souls are of divine nature and that during the rituals, they are appropriated by the medium in order to pronounce oracles or dictate blessings or curses on someone.

[12] Allan Kardec is the pen name of the French educator, translator, and author Hippolyte Léon Denizard Rivail (1804–1869). He is the author of five books known as the Spiritist Codification and is the founder of Spiritism. Rivail began his own investigation of psychic phenomena, mainly mediumship, with a compilation of a thousand questions given to ten mediums, all purportedly unknown to each other, documented their responses, and adapted them into a philosophy that he called Spiritism, which he initially defined as "a science that deals with the nature, origin, and destiny of spirits, and their relation with the corporeal world."

In the West, in the 1970s those who practiced so-called channeling, a form of New Age spiritism, claimed to be able to contact, through a channel, all the invisible entities, such as angels, gnomes, goblins, elves, fairies, spirits of nature, spirits of fire, spirits of water, and the great spirit of the earth. Clearly, this phenomenon of neo-paganism that is part of the New Age movement is winning over many lost and disoriented souls right now.

There are some who would simplify this broad phenomenology, which we have just sketched here in some of its particular forms, preferring to speak of parapsychology, projections of the unconscious, and other phenomena that have a psychological character with no effective correspondence in reality. My idea, however, is that these evoked spirits, if they are not the result of banal tricks, are none other than demons.

But first let us see what the Church says on the topic, beginning with the many passages from the Old Testament in which necromancy—the evocation of the dead—divination, and witchcraft are forbidden to the Israelites as superstitious practices that turn the heart away from faith in Yahweh, the providential God.[13] Then, in addition to the many pronouncements of the Magisterium throughout the centuries, there is also the *Catechism*, which says:

> All forms of *divination* are to be rejected: recourse to Satan or demons, conjuring up the dead or other practices falsely supposed to "unveil the future."[14] Consulting horoscopes, astrology, palm reading, interpretation of omens and lots; the phenomena of clairvoyance, and recourse to mediums

[13] Cf. Deut. 18:10–12; Lev. 19:31; 20:6.

[14] Cf. Deut. 18:10; Jer. 29:8.

> all conceal a desire for power over time, history, and, in the last analysis, other human beings, as well as a wish to conciliate hidden powers. They contradict the honor, respect, and loving fear that we owe to God alone. (CCC, no. 2116)

In light of this and of my long exorcistical practice, I believe that the evoked, presumed souls of the deceased (those that in precedence I called "roaming" or "wandering") are in reality unclean, awakened spirits, attracted, indeed "forced," by the evocation to manifest themselves. I also believe that to lead or simply to assist at such practices, even only occasionally, besides being a mortal sin, can provoke concrete and serious harm to the spirit. My agenda is full of appointments given to those who have consulted a medium. These individuals tell me that after such experiences, even long after, their problems increase: they have difficulty sleeping; they perceive some strange presences in their ambiences; they find it difficult to study; they experience a growing desire to commit suicide; they develop an unexplainable hatred toward others, and they become besieged by obsessive thoughts. Unfortunately the list could be lengthened to include the risks of contracting a serious spiritual evil such as a diabolical possession. The correlation between the cause and the diagnosis is so frequent that it is difficult for me to think that spiritism has nothing to do with the demon. The fact is, and I base this on the experience of all my colleagues in this ministry, that these evils are curable only through the medicine of the spirit: exorcism, blessings, prayer, and the sacraments; and this leads to the confirmation of all that I have said.

There are so many young people— I am speaking of twenty-five out of every hundred—who, together with their peers, either for a joke or out of boredom, get involved in these practices or participate at least once in their life at a séance. It is curious that, in a secularized and scientific era like ours, where anything credible must be experimentally demonstrated, so many people dive into these types of experiences that deal so strongly with the invisible world. The response is quite simple: when faith in God declines, idolatry and irrationality increase; man must then look elsewhere for answers to his meaningful questions. But there is another response that seems to me to go even deeper: a highly technical society accustoms individuals to obtain all that they wish by clicking a button, so they avail themselves of this method in order to obtain responses to the more difficult questions.

For clarity, I wish to further speak about two others types, namely sensitives and seers.[15] Like mediums or wizards, both can be braggarts or, worse, real witches or wizards. But there are also others [in this category] who are inspired to do good and sense or see spiritual realities. If they have a solid faith, and if they do not seek glory or gain, and if when tested they prove to be trustworthy, they can be very useful. I know some of them, and I employ them when it is helpful.

By going back to a photograph of a person, a letter, or an object, they can, with a certain precision, identify the existence of the spell and its origin, thereby permitting the identification and the destruction of the material cause. Furthermore, they can also assist in the selection of the most adaptable spiritual

[15] "The seers and sensitives have substantially the same characteristics. The first *see* and the second *feel;* both express what they have experienced through contact with objects or individuals." Gabriele Amorth, *An Exorcist Tells His Story*, 12th ed. (San Francisco: Ignatius Press, 1994), 157.

medicine to apply to a particular situation. In my experience, it has often happened that they can identify which parts of the victim's body to anoint—that is, where he was directly struck by the spell—or they can discern the time in which the person sustained the results of a rite.

Satanic Rock: The Collective Exaltation That Kills the Soul

Without a shadow of a doubt, the most diffuse method of transmitting the principles of Satanism is satanic rock. This makes Satanism live through music, which, in itself, is a common and beautiful form of entertainment. However, the Mephistophelian sound represents a great and actual danger for young people, who are the majority of those who are attracted to it and, in a certain sense, the most defenseless. In the messages that are transmitted through the sounds of satanic rock are the three rules of Satanism: you may do all that you wish, no one has the right to command you, and you are the god of yourself. Between the performances and the collective exaltation, created as entertainment and presented in a stadium, satanic rock very much mirrors the desires of young people.

Satanic rock's contagious music gives a sense of cheer, self-possession, and unlimited liberty from parents, teachers, and educators. If it is true that it is not necessary to see the devil everywhere, then for some this music is only a passion, although morbid; but it seems to me that the most devoted followers of this particular musical genre belong to satanic sects. So I advise everyone to avoid poisoning their spirits with these sounds.

Does one also risk diabolical possession by listening to this music? I have never had a case in which I was able, with great certainty, to recognize a possession caused by satanic rock. Nevertheless, I was able to ascribe other disturbances to it—none less painful—such as vexations or diabolical obsessions that provoke suicidal or homicidal inclinations. It is also necessary to remember that satanic rock spreads messages that are taken from the manuals of the black masses, spiritism, and occultism—in which Satan is evoked with musical lyrics that are actual hymns to the Prince of Darkness—and when they are projected onto a screen at concerts, they become, in a subliminal way, provocations of violence, suicide, sexual perversion, and acts of destruction against the state, the civic order, and the Church of God.

[Satanic rock] is a conditioning that overwhelms the external senses—sight and hearing—and arriving directly at the subconscious, erodes, over time, its inhibiting brakes. The obsessive repetition of these messages literally changes the way one thinks of and understands life, poisoning the soul and the spirit and, as a result, ruining lives.

Cursing: A Poisoning of the Environment

It is common knowledge that some people, even the young and little children, curse. But can these expressions, which often seem more like interjections than real offenses against God and our Lady, cause collateral damage in terms of evil spells? First of all, let us say that those who curse are in good company: the demoniacs (those possessed by the devil) often curse. Many persons, perhaps the majority, do not have a true awareness of the monstrosity they speak when they are cursing, offending the One who created them and insulting the Mother of the One who saved them. Rudeness, bad habits, and contagion accompany cursing. Furthermore, it is a grave sin that must be confessed.

Certainly, cursing is not at all displeasing to the devil. I personally have direct evidence of a cause-effect relationship between cursing and diabolical possession: I have been involved in cases regarding persons who contracted a diabolical possession or another evil spell caused by cursing. I also recall, without going too far, that it created a climate adaptable for similar phenomena. Certainly, apart from everything else, cursing ruins the climate of a home, which is the center of our lives.

What can we do when we hear someone cursing? I advise, in defense of a place or a family, to repeat in your mind a very short prayer; for example, "Jesus, I love You," or "Blessed be Jesus." This type of reparation is an effective retort against the devil, who, at that point, has more to lose than to gain from a curse.

Horror Films, Piercing, and Tattoos

What type of influence do books and especially horror films have on a spiritual life? A negative one. To read crime stories in the newspapers is to ask: Where does reality end and fantasy begin? At times there is a connection between the two, a reciprocal influence between what happens in life and what is born in the mind of writers and dramatists. I often wonder who inspires whom. I oppose the viewing of [horror] films, and I advise people, particularly the young, not to patronize them. If the demon's mission is to tempt man, then viewing these films—which tend to normalize brutal situations, particularly, where the demon is the protagonist—can seriously upset fragile minds and stir others to sadistic emulation. Why voluntarily subject oneself to evil temptations? The same regards similar content in animated cartoons and comics for boys and girls.

I must admit, however, based on my knowledge and experience, that the viewing of these films does not directly cause extraordinary spiritual ills. If anything, patronizing such films may influence a person to procure them indirectly or induce him to give himself over to occultism. Nevertheless, whoever contributes to the production and distribution of these films is, in every case, doing a disservice to society.

Tattoos? Piercing? These, as we know, are very common aesthetic practices among the young and the not so young. Tattooing and piercing—like nonsatanic rock—do not necessarily have an evil objective and do not in themselves demonize. Man, from time immemorial, has adorned his body. But I ask myself: Does adorning with indelible images on the skin embellish or disfigure the body, God's creation and therefore already beautiful in itself? In our view (as exorcists) it is always necessary to look at the intentions. Some of the symbolism and the designs on the body can make explicit or implicit referral to monsters or demons, nearly evoking them. At times one can associate these forms of expressions as signs of belonging to the devil: in this case, they are connected to the satanic rites of initiation. Other times, more simply, it is done to impress friends. Still other times, it can be done with explicit sexual references or to scorn one's own body. All these examples do nothing good for the soul. In a few cases, sacred images are represented: these are licit.

Ethnic Objects

A word about so-called ethnic objects: handmade African, Asian, or South American [objects], such as masks or other artifacts that are easily bought at open markets. Can they hide some evil influence? It is an interesting question, but one cannot give a definite response. Certainly there is a risk that an object of such a nature could have been part of a magic rite intended to harm the future possessors. Initially I would say not to dramatize it, above all if it was given as a gift with good and sincere intentions. A little vigilance, however, is not wasted.

At this point, I wish to summarize what I have already said about magic: it has very ancient origins, and it is present in practically every culture. Magic consists in the recourse to the preternatural, that is, to demonic forces, in order to influence human events to one's own advantage or to the detriment of someone else. Whoever practices it—from the wizard to the client—entrusts himself to the devil, which is a serious sin. Magic is either imitative or contagious. Imitative magic uses a form that in some way resembles the person on whom the rite is being carried out. For example, one punctures a puppet with a nail or a needle in order to strike the person the puppet represents. Here a type of transfer occurs from the object to the person. But magic of the contagious or infective type occurs through contact with objects that have belonged to the person, such as articles of clothing or other household items or by making the person ingest cursed foods. Whenever these objects have been cursed, they transfer their negative potential to the person.

Let us return to the African mask and to the other souvenirs from exotic places. They can hide a negative effect but do not necessarily do so. It is a risk and a danger, however, for anyone to buy them or accept them. I certainly would not wish to have them in my home. What tells us that they are cursed? Above all, when they inspire a sudden aversion toward the sacred. They also cause local disturbances: obscure presences, nauseating odors, unnatural noises, the persistence of negative physical symptoms on people, and [negative] personal and work-related situations. Therefore, it is a good rule to have these objects blessed. In the case of clearly self-evident problems, it is necessary to liberate oneself immediately from the object, either by burning it or by tossing it where water flows, such as a river, canal, or sea.

Do the Sins of Our Ancestors Affect Our Life?

Another theme that pops up, usually in a charismatic setting, is the so-called genetic tree. It is a controversial topic. There are those who maintain that the consequences of their ancestors' mediumism and particularly some of their serious sins—such as homicide, abortion, suicide, and magical practices—are passed on to successive generations. The same would be valid for their positive attitudes, such as courage and generosity. But here I am speaking of sins—not moral faults—and some of their consequences, which include a propensity, or an innate inclination, to repeat the same sinful acts. In other words, there could exist a generational transmission not only of physical and psychological traits, but also spiritual, such as particular sensibilities tied to serious sins or vices ascribable to ancestors and propagated from father to son. In brief, it would be a type of spiritual pollution that affects children, grandchildren, great-grandchildren and so on down the genealogical tree. To liberate oneself from these tendencies, each descendent would have to denounce them expressly through a Christian lifestyle and prayer life (in particular, prayers of deliverance), which would cut such ties. Once the sinful tendency was identified and a path of purification taken up, one's faults would be corrected and one's ways mended. Similarly, this would heal the transmission of the insanity characteristic from one generation to another.

This evocative thesis has been diffused through the book by the English psychiatrist Kenneth McCall entitled *Healing the Haunted* (1989), in which the author maintains—citing cases known to him—that the cause of evil spells can depend on genealogical questions. He also speaks of the "healing Masses" of the genealogical tree. These Masses are offered as intercession for the deceased who, because of their sins, still do not enjoy the light of God and are still in purgatory. In his book, McCall cites some episodes in which, after these charismatic Masses, the negative effects of the suffering souls on the living disappear. Apart from our beliefs on this matter, it is always opportune to celebrate Masses for our dear deceased, even those whom we have never known and who, perhaps, lived centuries ago.

Among exorcists there is no uniform position on the genealogical tree. Each one develops a personal position based on his considerable experience. I have had some cases in which persons suffering demonic possession had ancestors who practiced magic and witchcraft. Moreover, I have ascertained that a curse can be transmitted [from one generation to the next], particularly if it is issued by a father or a mother against a son, his marriage, and his future children. For many years I followed a youth who was cursed in the womb by his father; in fact, he was unwanted. And the father continued to curse him, so that, when he was grown, this unlucky youth had to deal with many misfortunes. He took good advantage of the blessings that he received from me and from other exorcists, but these had a limited effect. An even more glaring case was that of a young woman whose parents opposed her marriage to the young man of her choice. They cursed her on the very day of her marriage, wishing her the worst evils, and this was unfailingly accomplished. Only years of prayer alleviated the sorrows and the sufferings of this young family.

Alas! Curses, which are wishes of evil, are extremely powerful, especially if they are made with real treachery by those who are related by varying degrees of kinship to the victim. But they can be conquered with blessings. Jesus said, "[B]less those who curse you, pray for those who abuse you" (Luke 6:28).

In my view, there is not enough evidence to support the transgenerational thesis. My teacher, Father Candido Amantini, had serious doubts that sinful tendencies spread generationally. Moreover, would not the adherence to this hypothesis permit a person to abandon his sense of responsibility for his own life? But even with this doubt, I always advise the afflicted to make whatever sacrifices are necessary to break each evil spell.

4

The Extraordinary Action of Satan: Possession, Vexation, Obsession, and Infestation

Ordinary Diabolical Action: Temptation and Sin

Satan's mission is well explained by the apostle Peter: "Your adversary the devil prowls around like a roaring lion, seeking some one to devour" (1 Pet. 5:8). We can interpret that devouring as doing harm, bringing to perdition. The devil's mission in the world is to seduce souls, to lead each man and woman on the wayward paths of sin; and the principal path of this tragic mission is the path of temptation. Each one of us must fight against the temptation to sin for as long as we live. Indeed, sin leads to death.

It should not surprise anyone—and I shall speak of it shortly—if I say that there are more victims of Satan's ordinary action than of his extraordinary action. We are all victims of temptation, but only some are victims of the extraordinary action of Satan, but never through their own fault; therefore, they are not morally responsible. Temptation assaults us each holy day. Jesus Himself submitted to temptation during the forty days He spent in the desert after His baptism in the Jordan (see Matt.

4:1–11) and also later on. The devil tempts us both in our natural dimension, that is, in our interior wounds and weaknesses, and through the various occasions of sin that present themselves to us. Temptation is dangerous because it is difficult to uncover in the folds of our thoughts, words, works, and omissions. Discernment is necessary; that is, we must have a well-trained eye and the spiritual intelligence that helps us to recognize the claw of the tempter and those who bring us straight to sin; we must reject them and instead accept the good inspirations that come from God. Therefore, it is necessary to guard our heart and our external senses from indecent spectacles: each of us becomes what we see, what we listen to, and what we read. Therefore, let us be discerning in what we see and listen to, and above all let us choose good friends.

It is also necessary to have a well-formed conscience. A good conscience is not achieved by elevating oneself or, worse yet, allowing the dominant culture to arbitrate good and bad. A good conscience is obtained by conforming one's will to God's will and to His teachings, which are given to us for our happiness and our salvation and are summarized in the highest degree in the Commandments. The loss of a sense of sin that characterizes our era helps Satan to act nearly undisturbed and, inducing man to sin, takes man progressively away from the love of God: "Everything is lawful." "What wrong is there?" "Everyone does it." These are the suggestions that weaken the consciences of men and women and lead them on the paths toward closing their hearts, egoism, lack of forgiveness, and doing everything for money, power, and sex. Everything that seduces and enslaves souls leads to their death, which is Satan's objective.

The ordinary temptations of the devil are played mainly in the area of intelligence. Let us think of the many theoretical errors that are passed off as modern ideas in order to unhinge the principles of the Faith, as in all the new lifestyles that are contrary to morality: cohabitation, separation, divorce, betrayal, abortion, same-sex marriage, and euthanasia. Not to speak of corruption, wars, and egoism in all its innumerable forms. The list is truly long.

What is the cause of this moral decline? Principally it is the diminution of the Christian conscience in the struggle against the powers of darkness. It is St. Paul who warns us: "For we are not contending against flesh and blood, but against the principalities, against the powers, against the world rulers of this present darkness, against the spiritual hosts of wickedness in the heavenly places" (Eph. 6:12). Here is how Vatican II frames the situation:

> When the order of values is jumbled and bad is mixed with the good, individuals and groups pay heed solely to their own interests, and not to those of others. Thus it happens that the world ceases to be a place of true brotherhood. In our own day, the magnified power of humanity threatens to destroy the race itself.
>
> For a monumental struggle against the powers of darkness pervades the whole history of man. The battle was joined from the very origins of the world and will continue until the last day, as the Lord has attested [cf. Matt. 24:13; 13:24–30, 36–43]. Caught in this conflict, man is obliged to wrestle constantly if he is to cling to what is good, nor can he achieve his own integrity without great efforts and the help of God's grace.[16]

The martyrdom of so many Christians in the Near and Far East reminds us of this dramatic reality.

[16] *Gaudium et Spes*, no. 37.

The Extraordinary Action of the Devil

- *Diabolical possession.* Without a doubt, diabolical possession, the invincible influence of the devil on a person, is the most striking and serious form of the extraordinary action of the devil. When the demon is able to take possession of a person, he can make him say and do what he wishes. It is necessary to clarify that the devil is not able to take possession of the soul of a man (unless the person expressly consents to it), but only his body. Nevertheless, I must say that the cases of valid and true possession are rare: cases of vexation, obsession, and infestation, which I shall treat further on, are more frequent.

When possession is manifested, the obsessed goes into a trance and loses consciousness, leaving space for the evil spirit to speak; to agitate the person; to curse; to vomit nails, glass, or other objects; and to demonstrate herculean strength—in brief, to take over. On this subject Father Candido told me of the case of a young girl, an extremely thin and apparently weak demoniac who, during the exorcisms, had to be tied with leather straps and held firm, with difficulty, by four very energetic men. Well, she managed to break the straps with which they attempted to tie her, causing them much trouble until the end of the rite. It also happened to me: a decade ago, a very thin young girl—she could not have been more than thirteen years old—accompanied by her mother and her mother's friends, received incredible strength from the devil during an exorcism. It took all seven of my "guardian angels," the persons who accompany me with prayer, to hold her firm.

During these crises, the manifestation of abnormal phenomena occurs at intervals, but not continuously. The subject will lose consciousness all of a sudden. But at other moments of the day, [the subject] will appear normal. The possession is seldom permanent. More often the crises are provoked by external motives—for example, during a situation of spiritual stress, such as the exorcism itself, the Mass, benediction, prayer, or even the simple introduction of a sacred object. At other times, it goes off without apparent cause. The demon acts when, how, and where he wishes—during the day, at night, or even in a public situation, so that all can see. In these cases its will is acting through the spiritual power of its angelic nature. Nothing in these cases is ascribable to the victim of the possession.

In the case of the possessed person who has ingested cursed foods, he may, during the exorcism or during Mass, begin to cough spasmodically and spit dense saliva. In these circumstances it is helpful [for him] to ingest blessed or exorcized water, salt, and oil.

I have noticed that each possession is unique; this is also true for the other forms of the devil's extraordinary influence. There are liberations that occur in a few sessions and others that require many years of exorcisms. Some have obvious and coarse manifestations, and others—such as the case of a mute spirit—do not ever pronounce a word. These last are among the most difficult cases to treat.

Who becomes possessed? [People of every faith or none. The devil does not look in the face of anyone.] No one can consider themselves excluded: they can be young or old, believers or atheists, Christians or those of other religions. Through the years there have been Muslims who have had serious cases of possession. Not even consecrated religious are ruled out: I recall the case of Sister Angela, who was obsessed with a cursing that resounded in her mind. In most cases, those who are distant from the Faith are more susceptible to this risk, but this is only an indication of the maxim that says the devil is more tranquil if he does not have to live with prayer, fasting, the Eucharist, and the other sacramental practices.

I also add that the demon does not particularly like exercising his extraordinary action; he prefers by far to act through temptation. In the first case, the external manifestation clearly unmasks his existence. In the second, hiding himself behind ignorance and slight faith, he can act more easily because he is undisturbed. The devil is content when no one believes in his existence or when people consider him solely a medieval relic: then he is truly able to act tranquilly!

Temptation is conquered by vigilance, avoiding sin, and praying, because without the help of God we are not capable of conquering the seduction of sin. No one is exempt from temptation; some of the saints have had tremendous temptations even on their deathbeds. From their testimonies, we understand that as long as we have breath, we shall never be free of temptation.

It is useful to know that there are also multiple possessions; many spirits can be seen acting in a person contemporaneously. There was, for example, the case of Joanne, a woman of thirty, married with children. She fainted often and had severe headaches without apparent medical causes. In the course of various encounters, it was revealed that she was possessed by three demons who had entered through three spells, one of which was from a woman who aspired to have Joanne's fiancé before Joanne married him. The first two [demons] exited quickly and the third with more difficulty, but in the end we made it. It was a family of faith; for this reason, I believe, liberating Joanne was relatively simple.

There are cases, as in the Gospel of Mark, when Jesus was found with the demoniac possessed by a legion of devils (see Mark 5:1–20). This term, typical of the Roman military organization, suggests a reality that we exorcists often confront. When the possession is multiple, it has to do with spirits that are organized hierarchically, precisely like a military body: there are chiefs, deputy chiefs, and simple soldiers. Each one is provided with a different authority. Little by little, as the exorcism proceeds, the spirits with the least authority, the weaker spirits, abandon the field. The victory, the complete liberation, is accomplished after the defeat of the supreme head of the legion, the most powerful and overbearing, the last to leave the ship, the one of whom the other demons have a true and proper terror.

How does one discover that he is possessed? There are persons who discover they are possessed when frequenting a sacred place, perhaps a Marian sanctuary, or when they participate in retreats, processions, prayer encounters, or Eucharistic adoration. They may have had some disturbance in the past to which they didn't pay much attention, but then on those occasions it manifested itself in a clearer and more obvious way. It is the sign that the devil has remained hidden as long as he was able (he can hide himself for long periods, dissimulating his presence), but when confronting the power of God [during the exorcism] he must manifest himself. This fact, contrary to what one may think, must be accepted as a grace, because only in knowing the illness can one intervene.

This is also true for the other disturbances that we shall speak of shortly. At times, as mentioned in the case of Joanne, there are physical problems that medical doctors cannot explain, and then a bell goes off. It was like this for Marcella, a girl of nineteen who suffered from a stomach ailment and could not sleep, and who would give sharp answers at home and at work. As soon as I touched her, lifting her eyelids, her eyes were entirely white and the pupils reverted toward the back.[17] I did not even have time to

[17] "Almost always in cases of evil presence, the eyes look completely white; we can barely discern, even with the help of both

think when an evil sneer said to me: "I am Satan." We were able to liberate her in two years, but she is still much engaged in prayer.

I wish to stress that neither possessions nor evil spells are contagious. In other words, there is no risk of being struck by coming in visual, auditory, or tactical contact with demoniac persons. A demoniac can also marry and have children without danger of infecting her family. I say this, above all, to benefit the relatives and friends who may be asked to involve themselves in these difficulties and to stay close to these suffering persons with a prayerful and understanding attitude. At times, living with such people is very difficult and truly tests a person. This is even truer for the priest. We have already revealed that the more we fear the devil, the more he attacks us. Therefore, if we leave him alone he will become aware of our weakness and will never leave us in peace.

It is therefore true that persons who have had an experience with possession and then resolved it acquire a great sensibility toward situations in which a satanic presence is evident.

- *Diabolical vexation.* Diabolical vexations are the second type of the demon's extraordinary spiritual aggression and are far and away the most numerous. They are caused by a person's cultivation of imprudent habits; by frequenting wizards or séances, through repeated and persistent serious sins, or by submitting to spells. Here the devil acts without any dominant and prevailing influence over the body and the mind of the victim, as happens

---

hands, whether the pupils are toward the top or the bottom of the eye. The position of the pupils indicates the type of demons and troubles that are present. During questioning, we could always classify the types of demons according to a distinction inspired by chapter 9 of the book of Revelation." Amorth, *An Exorcist Tells His Story*, 78–79.

in the case of possession. Vexations are true and actual aggressions, physical or psychological attacks that the demon works against a person. At times they result in scratches, burns, bruises, or, in the most serious cases, broken bones. At times the victim is the target of stones or other objects. Typical cases of vexation are illnesses without any apparent cause that affect the internal organs or the limbs or pathologies that provoke pain in a part of the body without visible signs. Vexations can involve health, affections, or work.

Often the vexation is associated with an extraordinary evil spell, in the sense that the person possessed or obsessed can also exhibit physical and psychic disturbances. It happened to me that in liberating a demoniac, the woman was contemporaneously cured of a terrible tumor. Evidently in this case the spell submitted to by the demon had a duplicate effect, spiritual and physical. On the other hand, the Gospel also attests to cases of physical healing that are tied to a spiritual healing from an evil spell. For example, Jesus heals a mute demoniac (see Matt. 9:32–34) and a blind and mute demoniac (Matt. 12:22–24).

Vexations can also involve an oneiric dimension: while sleeping, a person may have terrible nightmares, in which he dreams of cursing, of damning God, or of becoming perverse and wicked. In this case, we are at the borders of diabolical obsession.

We can give some examples from the lives of the saints: St. Pio, for example, was whipped by a demon. The Curé of Ars was often thrown out of his bed by Satan. I would say that these cases concerned diabolical vexations, not possessions.

As I have said, vexations are not always manifested on a physical level. Sometimes they can strike affections: it can happen, for example, that a couple who are married or are engaged to be married can separate, or, to the contrary, two persons can become engaged, even though they are incompatible. Other vexations are manifested in work: the person in search of it does not find it; or the person who finds work loses it; or a person may have gross difficulties with colleagues and bosses at work. Other times, [vexations] can break up friendships and isolate a person. It is impossible to enumerate all the cases.

How does one distinguish between a physical illness and a diabolical vexation? It is necessary, as always, to be very prudent in evaluating symptoms. People who are easily impressionable can become upset without foundation. Often, in fact, an illness or psychological discomfort is natural and can be easily diagnosed by a medical or psychiatric specialist. But anyone who notices the presence of tormenting phenomena tied to an inexplicable aversion to the sacred, to God, or to prayer should seek spiritual discernment. Likewise, having frequented occult practices in the past or contacted wizards, mediums, or fortune-tellers, even in good faith, or having been subjected to spells can be valid indications for the need for good discernment.

- *Diabolical obsession.* Diabolical obsessions are disturbances or extremely strong hallucinations that the demon imposes, often invincibly, on the mind of the victim. In these cases the person is no longer master of his own thoughts. Rather, he is subjected to a powerful force that creates mental activity in him that is repetitive, obsessive, and irresistible. Such representations of reality, even if foreign to his manner of thinking, become profoundly fixed in his psyche. The objects of these hallucinations can be manifested as visions, as voices, or as rustlings; they can also appear as monstrous figures, horrifying animals, or devils. In other cases it can be an impulse to commit suicide or to do evil to others; and, particularly in the young, it can lead to confusion about one's gender. The history of cases is so vast that it is impossible to enumerate all the forms of diabolical obsession.

This usually does not completely deactivate the mind and the will of a person, who remains conscious and alert. It does, however, heavily condition him in his relationship with the world. This phenomenon can occur indifferently at night or during the day, and experiencing it can make one's life impossible, even to the point of suicide. For obvious reasons this situation provokes sadness and desperation in the victim.

Even the saints are not exempt from diabolical obsessions: when the demon appeared to St. Pio of Pietrelcina, he assailed St. Pio like a ferocious dog or disguised himself as his spiritual director with special instructions. In order to avoid every misunderstanding, it is necessary to state precisely that these obsessive disturbances are very similar to mental pathologies; and for this reason, it is always necessary to seek the help of a psychiatrist in order to determine if it is a natural illness. Given the difficulty of judging this classification of cases, a conversation with a priest, in his capacity as a spiritual adviser, can also be very helpful. In fact, it often happens that the clinical results of a demoniac pathology have psychiatric counterparts. In this case, it is necessary to proceed at the same rate with both, joining the medical treatment with the spiritual. We shall speak of this in more depth.

- *Diabolical infestation.* We come to the last type of spiritual disturbances—diabolical infestations: disturbances that act on houses, objects, and animals, rather than on people.[18] It does not mean

[18] "The Bible does not menion any exorcism of houses, but experience demonstrates that in certain instances this is necessary and fruitful. It is true that, at the end of the exorcism of Leo XIII,

that they produce less suffering in the individuals who are associated with this satanic action. Indeed, the infestation of the house, in particular, provokes great sufferings and, at times, enormous economic damage to the property and to the one subjected to it. In these cases, the demons can damage electrical appliances, automobiles, and home-heating systems.

There are other examples of infestations: doors and windows that open and slam shut, day and night, without any apparent causes; lights, lamps, televisions, or computers that turn on and shut off without any human intervention; detonators that go off; the sound of footsteps; violent vibrations, mysterious voices or cries; and powerful blows to the walls, all of which can make life difficult for the inhabitants. In some of my cases, the police were called in order to verify the presence of strong blows, but always without finding the culprit. Still more: there can be stones tossed against windows, but without the glass breaking; intense unpleasant odors; or the invasions of insects, such as cockroaches or ants, that can be so aggressive that they erode windows frames in just a few days. Here also the case history is vast.

In such cases, it is necessary to determine whether the phenomenon is concretely attributable to natural and certifiable causes. If not, it is useful to know—although it is often difficult to verify—if in the past séances or magic rituals were held in the house, or gatherings of Masonic or satanic sects, or anything similar. Also in these cases, it is useful to have the house and its contents blessed and to have local exorcisms (on the property),

---

we ask a blessing for the place where these prayers are recited, but the prayer itself is an invocation for God's protection over the Church against the evil spirits, with no mention of places." Amorth, *An Exorcist Tells His Story*, 123.

which in these circumstances can be very long and complicated. In the worst cases, I have had to advise the occupants to change houses. At times, in the new home there are no more strange occurrences. At other times, the disturbances continue.

For example, I recall the case of a person whose bed would move, often violently, when she was lying down. I asked her whether the same disturbance presented itself when she was sleeping away from the house. She responded that wherever she went, the phenomenon manifested itself. Evidently, here, it involved a personal vexation. In other situations, the disturbances go away.

Therefore, it is important to verify if, in changing the bed or the house, the disturbance passes. If so, this means that the spell is tied to the bed, the house, the room, or the wall. But when a person always experiences the same disturbances, then the problem resides in the person, and it is he who needs to act: with an exorcism, prayer, and a sacramental life.

The Risk of Liberty

We have spoken of evil spells: possession, vexation, obsession, and infestation. Now the question arises: Why does God permit evil?

First, it is necessary to make clear that God, being infinite love, does not wish evil. He simply permits it, because He created men and angels as free creatures. Simply put, men are free to choose whether they wish to live for God or against Him and therefore to opt for heaven or for hell. We must recognize that God has made everything to make man happy, and in accordance with this plan, God asks man to obey the laws that He has established; but God has also given man the ability to refuse this truth. This is the situation in which all of us are placed.

The first who had to choose, as we have already said,[19] were the angels, who, in the case of the demons, chose to tempt men in order to attract men to themselves. The second, in the dimension of time, is man; and so it falls to each of us individually to make a choice. John's Gospel says of Christ: "[A]ll things were made through him, and without him was not anything made that was made" (John 1:3). Could God have given to creation a greater goal than Himself, than the possibility of enjoying the vision of Him, the cause of eternal joy? We, in fact, live for Him, and there could not be a more marvelous goal. Therefore, the rebellion of the angels and the successive disobedience of men tells us that evil is a concrete possibility and that God has permitted it in order to make us free.

And here we are before a great mystery: that creatures freely choose evil rather than good. It was the case of Joseph, a youth of twenty-eight, who emanated a strong odor of smoke and who used and sold drugs and cursed. I could see immediately that he came to me solely to please his mother and his sister, who accompanied him. I had just begun to pray when the demon manifested itself immediately and violently, and I had to stop. When [Joseph] recovered, after the exorcism, I told him that he was possessed. He told me that he already knew that he was demoniac and that he was fine with it. I never saw him again.

This is the greatest risk that God has taken with His creatures, angels and men. And He has taken it for a simple reason: because without free will, that is, without the possibility of choosing between good and bad, we would be robots and not totally free creatures. Liberty—infinite in God—is a sign of our greatness and of our sonship in Jesus Christ. Without it, we could not call

[19] See chapter 3.

ourselves sons, but only slaves. God has given us everything; we must recognize only Him, adore only Him, and be guided only by Him, because inevitably, if we do not give to God, we necessarily give to idols. "He who is not with me is against me," Jesus says (Matt. 12:30). Half measures do not exist. Either we are of Christ, or we are of Satan. At times we would like to go halfway: serving Christ partway. Well, this is not possible. The devious method that the devil used with Adam and Eve works also with us: it leads us to think that evil and sin do not exist, that to sin, distancing ourselves from God, trying each thing for the pleasure of having experiences, is a gain. "So, in the end, what evil is there?"

At times, in order to console my clients who have been tried by long years of possession, I remind them that if they have found the faith to begin a true Christian life, it is because they had to begin a hard struggle against the evil that they were suffering. As a result, the devil was already defeated at the start.

It is true that God permits evil, but there is another truth that accompanies it: without our knowing, God also puts a limit on evil, limiting the action of Satan against man. We have an example of it in the book of Job; Satan obtains permission to vex Job, but God forbids him to touch Job: "Behold, all that he has is in your power; only upon himself do not put forth your hand" (Job 1:12). God always has the last word.

Permit me a last word of encouragement to those who suffer from evil spells, in particular to those who have contracted them through no fault of their own. My founder, Blessed Don Giacomo Alberione, always insisted on making reparation for sins through one's own suffering and the offering of one's suffering for the salvation of sinners and for peace in the world. Rather than nurturing a profound sense of pain and stirring up possible retaliatory thoughts, one can offer up to God a great and meritorious work.

How Are Spiritual Evils Contracted?

How does one contract the spiritual evils that we have just briefly described? In two ways: through sin and without sin.

Let us confront the first, which I call culpable because it results from a person's fault or sin. For example, many cases of possession are manifested—often after much time—when a person tries to resolve a personal problem, often work related or emotional, and turns to a wizard or, when practical, to forms of occultism in all its multiple styles; or when, often at a young age, and only as a joke, he may have played around with spiritism. As I have explained, when we speak of magic, we mean the use of negative spiritual forces in order to dominate the physical and psychological. It involves the manipulation of some preternatural powers for one's own ends; actions and attitudes that are harshly condemned in the Bible, for example: spells (see Exod. 7:11; Ps. 58:5); divination (see Gen. 30:27; Isa. 8:19); necromancy or spiritism (see Lev. 19:31; 1 Sam. 28:3ff.); witchcraft (see 2 Chron. 33:6; Jer. 27:9; Gal. 5:20); false prophets (see Ezek. 13:17–23); and sorcery (see Micah 5:12).

Another culpable means of contracting spiritual evils that in some cases can be particularly weighty is perseverance in sin and vice; that is, living a life—stubbornly and with conviction—that is contrary to love.

Are those who give themselves over to occultism or who live in serious sin always attacked by evil spells? Evidently not. We are not in the field of the medical sciences in which everything, or at least much, is measurable. There are no automatic mechanisms in either case. What I intend to say is that an evil spell does not necessarily attack a person who has taken up a vice or who turns to magic or occultism or to necromancy. Let us say, however, that whoever practices these vices places himself in great danger.

Are some vices more dangerous than others? I would not exclude any of them; in my experience, however, the most diffuse are the spiritual ills that are tied to an unrestrained use of sex. I recall, for example, a youth who was given over to much perverse sex, and because of this he was struck by a possession. I engaged many years and many exorcisms to liberate him. Other vices exist that have become ever more common today; those that I would call vicious and which at one time were favored solely by horror films and are now tranquilly presented on television or at the cinema. This promotion of evil has normalized the most inhuman cruelty, and many, unfortunately, aspire to it, if not always in behavior, at least in thought. But I repeat: I would not limit myself to these vices. I think of the unrestrained use of alcohol and drugs that is so diffuse among young people.

There are also blameless causes, which are decidedly the majority of the cases. In fact, I think that at least 90 percent of the cases of possessions and of other evil spells are directly attributable not to their victims but to those persons who have turned their particular attentions on them, practicing some spells or evil eye against them for various motives, such as resentment, hatred, or vendetta.

It may shock some that even a newborn or a young baby can be possessed by a demon, but it is the pure (and terrible) reality with which we exorcists must often deal. Evidently, here, we find ourselves before a blameless cause. It can happen that a spell does damage to the fetus of a pregnant woman, with the possible result that the newborn already presents problems at birth, even if, in all probability, those problems are not manifested consciously until [the child reaches] the age of reason. It also happens that a baby may be consecrated to Satan at a very tender age, often as a condition to participate in a ritual or a black mass.

Regarding this topic I am reminded of the case of Francesco Vaiasuso, whose story was publicized in a fascinating book.[20] This man, who is now over forty years old, was only four—and therefore too young to remember any of it—when he was subjected to a spell by drinking the blood from a black mass. He had been led to the mass by a presumed friend of the family without his mother's knowledge. This dramatic circumstance was discovered much later when he manifested an extremely strong possession. Francesco worked many years to liberate himself from the twenty-seven legions of demons that possessed him. Thanks to years of exorcism, an extraordinary wife, a life of prayer, and many prayers of deliverance, he made it, and today he has become a witness of these horrendous realities that strike man. What had he done to merit such a misfortune?

I also happened to have a case in which two friends were preparing for a competition together. One of the two knew that his companion was better prepared and probably had a better chance of success. So, evidently out of jealousy, he had a witch prepare an evil spell so that his friend would fail and he would succeed. Things went exactly like that: paradoxically the competition was won by the one who was less prepared, while the other, besides losing, found himself with an ugly possession. It is, unfortunately, a common occurrence.

[20] See Francesco Vaiasuso and Paolo Rodari, *La mia possessione. Come mi sono liberato da 27 legioni di demoni* (Milan: Piemme, 2013).

As I have already outlined, other cases involve the world of sentiments: the use of the evil eye to break up a marriage and rob a person of his or her legitimate spouse or, on the contrary, the use of magic potions to create sentimental ties that result in a marriage. To this last proposal the victim is always unaware and is thus dominated by the wife or the husband, who will then sever the victim's ties with the family of origin. Evidently, in this case, the marriage is null—although certainly difficult to demonstrate—because it was obtained through subterfuge. What can be done to repair such a situation? Above all, the person must open his eyes before some of the clamorous facts of his family life, perhaps with the help of friends and priests. Only then can he begin the path to liberation, which always begins with personal prayer.

Another question regards the sex and the age of those who most often turn to exorcists—in my experience, women and young people. For the young people, the response is easy: their curiosity often pushes them to go beyond the limits of prudence, and they end up in the myriad tentacles of occultism. For the women, it seems more complex: among the causes I would indicate, they have, unlike the majority of men, a greater propensity to turn to the Church in cases of need. Certainly it can also be the awareness on the part of the demon that the women are the more delicious bite, because, once the woman is conquered, he often has the entire family in his hands. Did not the ancient serpent do the same with Eve?

The Daily Life of the Possessed Person

What is the daily life of a demoniac like? The cases are very diverse. As I was saying, normally the state of possession—the strange behavior stirred up by a crisis—can be manifested by a simple change of tone or by the evident aversion to the sacred that is evidenced by cursing and blaspheming—but these situations do not last the entire day. Often demoniacs behave normally; many of them go to work, where their colleagues are oblivious of their situation. At times, however, these persons, even when they do not fall into an evident state of possession, are subjected to interior assaults by the Evil One that are difficult to control. I am speaking of legs that tremble or become immobilized, of abdominal pains, headaches, sudden mood changes, and other various ailments. Thus, they learn to develop various strategies of behavior that help them to overcome the various crises without attracting too much attention; for example, going into a restroom until everything becomes normal again. There are, however, more serious cases, in which a person is impeded from having any type of professional or social life.

What triggers a crisis? Often the awareness of a problem is caused by an aversion to the sacred, such as contact with the Eucharist, even just visual, or an exorcistical prayer or simply entering a church or a sanctuary. In other cases, an easily decipherable cause does not exist. When an evil spell has been provoked by the culpable behavior of the person struck, however, the crises are usually more serious. Often these persons have collateral consequences throughout their lives, even after they have experienced liberation. Therefore, it is necessary to put people, especially young people, on guard against giving themselves over to occultism. As verified each day, the consequences are very serious.

The persons who are prey to spiritual evils are not necessarily impeded from going to Mass or from praying. Each case is different. Some participate at the Eucharistic celebration without particular problems. Others manifest evident signs of a malaise that is reaching the state of possession. I do not say anything new if I confirm that there are priests who suffer from spiritual evils and that, in spite of it, they celebrate the Mass every day (although with difficulty). Regarding this last circumstance, there is nothing to marvel at. I follow young priests who, having just entered the seminary, were subjected to satanic rites on the part of persons opposed to their choice of the consecrated life; some are their own family members and, in one case, the deluded ex-fiancée. Some [of these men] renounce their vocation. Those who, to the contrary, hold firm exercise their ministry with difficulty but also with great efficacy. Their cases almost never involve a true and proper possession; usually it is a vexation or an obsession.

Life after Liberation from the Demon

Thanks be to God, there are many persons who have been liberated from the devil. Regarding this, the *Ritual of Exorcism* counsels: "It is advised that the faithful, once liberated, either alone or with family members, give thanks to God for the peace they have obtained. May it stay with them as long as they persevere in prayer, read the Sacred Scripture, receive the sacraments of Penance and the Eucharist, and practice a Christian life rich in charity, good works and fraternal love." The tasks of the ministry of liberation are not met solely with the loosening of ties to Satan. It is necessary that the Christian community, with the proper discretion, help the liberated brother or sister to proceed on his Christian journey; and the liberated person, on his part, is called to undertake joyously such a path through a life of sanctity, animated by charity.

In my experience, once a person is released — at times, after years of exorcism and prayers and not a few moments of discomfort — he usually does not have any permanent effects: he returns to his daily life, his relationships, and his work in a normal way.

Indeed, he often understands that his new situation is a true and proper gift from God, asked for with insistence and at the end obtained. After this experience he develops a sense of gratitude toward Jesus, toward our Lady, and toward the saints; and his faith is stronger than ever.

Often such persons are given the grace to help those who find themselves still immersed in the effects of demonic attacks. Thus, they become apostles in the true sense of the word, giving testimony to what they have lived, in prayer groups, in their parishes, or in any other occasions that may arise spontaneously. The most impressive case, already mentioned, is that of Francesco Vaiasuso. Today, along with the commercial activity that he manages in his town in Sicily, he tours Italy giving his testimony, exercising his ministry of liberation, and holding well-attended conferences.

To Whom Does One Turn in Case of Doubt?

When signs appear that could be considered the results of an evil spell, my first advice, always, is to address the concerns to a psychiatrist. When one is ill, the first thought should be of natural causes that can be treated with traditional medicine. In fact, only rarely does an illness have a diabolical origin. Normally, one should have recourse to an exorcist only as a second response. I say this for the benefit of persons who are very impressionable. I myself do not accept anyone—except in clear cases—if I do not first have a psychiatric diagnosis.

What do I mean by clear cases? For example, a long time ago, a father, very religious and practicing, came to see me. His eighteen-year-old son had come home one day and, to everyone's surprise, began to curse and to destroy all the sacred images that he found around the home. The youth no longer went to church, and he would interrupt the prayer before meals with unheard-of verbal violence. Everyone was stunned by this change. Opposition to the sacred is one of the clearest signs of evil spells, and there is no need to have a medical opinion in order to begin treatment immediately.

Returning to the norm: after the person has gone to a psychiatrist, if the treatment turns out to be useless and if medical doctors are not able to make a diagnosis because they are convinced that they are before an unknown illness — in fact, many of them cannot even imagine the existence of evil spirits— then one can turn to a priest for advice. I recall the case of Mark, a boy whom I exorcized for a long time, who was struck by an extremely strong possession. The poor boy underwent heavy psychiatric treatment, including electric shock and a treatment for insomnia (he never slept): for an entire week he was given enough sleep medication to sedate an elephant, but he never slept, day or night. It was only after a long spiritual cure that he was liberated from his evil.

The opposite case happened to me with a woman who came to me for a blessing. She suffered from a pathology that had been treated by a neurologist for many years (and also some exorcists), but to no advantage. After questioning her, I realized that I could proceed with an exorcism. At the beginning, she had some strong reactions, and then she fell down and lost consciousness. When she revived, she insisted that she wanted a true exorcism, one that began with the words "I exorcise you" (evidently she had already heard them during an exorcism that was done to her). After she calmed down, she complained that just touching her made her eyes hurt. These are not attitudes typical of the possessed. When she returned for the next appointment she did not know if the exorcism had had any effect. Before dismissing her case, because I still had some doubts, I brought her to Father

Candido. After putting his hand on her head, he understood that there was nothing there that concerned demons; it was a psychiatric problem.

Where do you turn when you have suspicions of a demonic influence? You turn to your pastor or religious, who have some awareness of this type of reality. In fact, it often happens that persons who experience and suffer from evil spells are treated with little patience because they are considered crazy. Before judging them, priests should simply recite a prayer or give them a blessing and see what happens. At times, such a person will immediately give obvious signs of malaise. These reactions indicate that the person must turn to an exorcist.

There are also dubious cases in which the nature of the illness is not clear. Here it is opportune for psychiatrists and exorcists to work together. Indeed, a psychiatrist may work cooperatively with an exorcist even if he is not a believer; all that is necessary is that he recognize, at least in theory, that science, at times, can do nothing. In this way a fruitful collaboration can be established that is helpful to the person who is suffering; in practice, however, this is very rare.

Let us consider one last observation about the distinction between a psychiatric illness and the extraordinary influence of the demon. St. Pio of Pietrelcina was convinced that many persons who were admitted to psychiatric hospitals and who remained there during their entire natural life, were, in reality, possessed by the demon, and an exorcism would have been enough to cure them. This is also confirmed by the great apostle of psychiatric illnesses, the Spanish Carmelite Francis Palau. In the hospital in which he worked, he exorcised all the patients, curing many of them. This tells us something interesting: psychiatric symptoms and diabolical symptoms assume very similar forms. Therefore, knowing how to discern the true nature of evil is decisive in resolving the problem.

The Decisive Contribution of the Person Possessed

At times I am asked if a person without faith can be liberated from a demon solely with the prayers of others. Surely a Christian community, family members, and friends can open the path toward the cure, beseeching God for the grace of conversion for that person. But the liberation cannot ever occur against the will of the person possessed and without his effective contribution, that is, without the support of the sacraments and prayer.

How can a person without faith ask the Most High to liberate him from the influence of the devil? God does not force anyone to accept His gifts. In order to liberate oneself, it is necessary to live in the grace of God, to pardon the one who has done evil, to eradicate vices, and to break those human ties that keep him close to the Evil One. It is a great but absolutely necessary commitment: exorcists, like the prayers of deliverance, do not have any effect on a person who does not live in God's grace. In fact, I am convinced that a good confession, which is a very powerful sacrament, is much more efficacious than an exorcism, which, as we shall see, is only a sacramental.

A person also may not wish to be exorcized or receive a prayer. Obviously, one cannot force the person physically, but it is necessary to remember that it is often the evil spirit that is suggesting it, at times invincibly. It may happen that the person comes to the exorcism accompanied by relatives or with his pastor and that the spirit makes him fall into a trance before the prayer, perhaps solely at the sight of the undersigned as they are about to enter my study. In this case, the person is escorted with sweet firmness and subjected to the exorcism, since when he was conscious he had agreed to receive it. Often at the end of the rite he appears nearly defogged, and once again in possession of his volitional faculties. This is a confirmation that the prayer has obtained its effects; these effects, however, may be temporary, in the sense that the definitive liberation has not yet occurred and from here, for some time yet, he may go back to his listless state or to his aversion toward the sacred. But this defogging is a good sign: the person has reentered into himself, sensing that the path has been laid out and that it is only necessary to walk it.

Another great risk, perceived by those who suffer from evil spells, is that of remaining alone, isolated, and without support. Those who live the extraordinary demonic action often find themselves isolated and stigmatized by those who should be close and welcoming: relatives, acquaintances, and, as I have said often, even the ministers of Christ. Therefore, the spiritually ill often find themselves in a condition akin to the lepers of the Bible, estranged and marginalized. But Jesus, before the leper who prostrates himself and asks Jesus to purify him, extends His hand, touches him, and says to him: "I will; be clean" (Matt. 8:2–3). Just as the leper's wounds are evident in the body, the spiritual evils are manifested at a psychophysical level. In such a situation, the one who is spiritually wounded often has an aversion to the sacred that prevents him from finding comfort in moments of prayer or living the Mass in a composed manner. The truly spiritually ill are often convinced that they are crazy, and this thought is shared by many others, including family members, friends, and priests. As a result, the sick person is always being distanced from ordinary situations and lives constantly in the extraordinary, punctuated by exorcisms, prayers of deliverance, and searches for charismatics.This spiritual overexposure is in itself a danger because it encloses the person in a ghetto and isolates him.

The greatest challenge is normalizing the abnormal and making the extraordinary ordinary. How is it done? By following the sequence taught by Jesus with the lepers, by actively offering attention, compassion, and acceptance to the person suffering tribulation; surrounding him with both laymen and priests who are capable of competent and empathetic listening; and suffering with the victim. It is also necessary to provide places for social gatherings and moments of acceptance, where they can pray together, laugh, and learn how to share, to suffer, and also to be joyful. Finally, it is necessary to help the one who is suffering to put a personal action plan into motion so that he can take control of his illness and of the Evil One, so that the Evil One does not have the final word.

In Italy an association that has formed recently and that seems very promising is the Family of the Light with Camilla,[21] which promotes the acceptance of persons who suffer from spiritual evils and offers courses in sensitization and awareness. It is open to the clergy and the laity, and many have found its assistance valuable.

When the Family Is Attacked by a Demon

We conclude this chapter by focusing on the actions of Satan on families. Today families are among the most targeted by the ordinary action of Satan, through the chilling of relationships as well as betrayals and divisions. Unfortunately families are not exempt from the extraordinary action of Satan, even if it is only a single member who has been struck by an evil spell. It may

[21] See the website: www.famigliadellaluce.it.

happen that there is more than one victim; in these cases, the spell has been repeated or in some way extended to affect others. Most often, the hatred of the one who commissioned the spell is aimed at all the family members in order to strike a single component. In such cases, it is indispensable that each member, even the one who seems exempt or less likely to be struck, frequent the sacraments and apply himself with greater engagement in prayer. It is also opportune to receive benedictions and to address them not only to the persons being struck but also to their homes. Another practice is to make use of sacramentals, such as making the Sign of the Cross with blessed water before going to bed or right after getting up. It is also a good rule to keep sacred images on one's person or to display them in the house. Statues of the Holy Family or saints inspire us to imitate their virtue and remind us to ask for protection in prayer. If one is able to have a Mass celebrated in the home and to recite prayers of deliverance, this can only help. Obviously, in the most serious cases, it is necessary to see an exorcist. I also believe that, on the strength of the efficacy that is derived from the sacrament of marriage, each spouse can implement repeated prayers of deliverance on the other spouse and on the children.

Regarding this, I recall a family that, in a brief time, went to rack and ruin: the father, a businessman, lost all his orders due to some strange circumstances; a daughter was left with children by her husband, and the other daughter was left by her fiancé shortly before their wedding; and at home there were strange noises. With a Mass, an exorcism in their home, and a benediction on the members of that family, the disturbances disappeared.

One of the most glaring cases I ever had is that of Lucia and Francesco, a couple from Northern Italy who came to interview me. Nearly casually, during the encounter we discovered that the husband was possessed by a demon. We managed to liberate him in a brief time, but then the daughter soon manifested problems; and then the same thing, although less seriously, occurred to Lucia and to the second child. For the manner in which they were hammered and the courage they demonstrated in relating their story in a book, which I highly recommend,[22] it seems to me to be an emblematic case of how to confront a spiritual battle with the demon: with everyone united, in spite of all the difficulties—and for them there were many (and there still are!)—and with much prayer.

Finally, I would like to give two simple recommendations to young married couples. The first is to develop immediately the habit of praying together. This will lead to greater harmony and will keep away many evils. The second is to extend this good habit to your children and bring them to church—even when they are little and even if they cry and run around the church. One is educated in the church through osmosis. They will be grateful when they are grown, and so will you. And one must not omit—even if it is difficult—the desire of pardon toward the one who has acted wickedly against him.

[22] Lucia e Francesco, *A tu per tu con il diavolo. Una famiglia perseguitata dal Maligno* (San Paolo: Cinisello B., 2009).

5

Body to Body with Satan: The Exorcism

The First Step: Dealing with the Doubters

When dealing with the extraordinary manifestations of Satan—possession, vexation, obsession, and infestation—who is qualified to verify the existence of the evil spells? It is necessary to be very prudent when discerning if one is dealing with a problem that has an evil origin. As I have said, once it is ascertained that it does not involve a pathology of a psychiatric nature, it is appropriate to turn to a priest, possibly one prepared in this matter. Also groups of the Catholic Charismatic Renewal can be of great help in this first phase of evaluation. If guided by qualified persons gifted with good sense, they can help to make detections through charismatic public prayer.

Regarding the priests, my confreres: What attitude must they demonstrate toward a person who says he is suffering from a spiritual evil? By the nature of his ministry, the ordained minister reflects qualities of acceptance, listening, and consolation. If we think of the persons the Lord encountered, we see how many asked to be accepted and listened to and only then to be cured. We think of the blind man cured at Bethsaida whom we find in the Gospel of Mark (see Mark 8:22–26). Jesus took him by his hand, making him feel His closeness and His love. Then he cured him. He does the same with the demoniacs: when He meets these persons who are suffering in the spirit, He frees them, giving a concrete sign that the Kingdom of God He announced at the beginning of the Gospel of Mark (Mark 1:15) has arrived with its work: the ousting of Satan. It is the paternal experience of God that touches each man and each woman; and each priest is called to do the same: to accept everyone, to listen, and to console.

Counseling the doubtful—and among these the persons who feel that they are affected by a diabolical possession or by another spiritual evil—is one of the Spiritual Works of Mercy to which each Christian is called. The desire to be touched by God, above all when one is suffering, indicates the desire to be visited by Him. And God responds quickly to the one who is moved by this longing. The desire that we feel toward God is our way of expressing our need for a relationship with the One who consoles us, curing us and revealing to us the sense of our existence. Living for God and with God is the mystery that He will reveal to us in its fullness only on the last day. We priests are asked, through our preaching, to communicate this mystery, but at the same time, assisted by a life fortified by prayer, we are asked to listen and to console; and at the end of our days, all the good that has passed through our hands, our eyes, and our mouth will be revealed to us.

Naturally this is also valid for the exorcist, who has the task of accepting and curing the brothers and sisters who are affected by spiritual evils. He must be a counselor who is always aware and willing to welcome the most disparate cases. In fact, it often happens that the persons who turn to him are truly desperate and no longer know which way to turn. Therefore, his first task is to verify each case with expertise and prudence. Only after he carries out this ministry of acceptance, consolation, and reassurance will he be able to ascertain the real presence of the evil and proceed with the exorcism.

I frequently encounter persons who are desperately seeking verification of a possession so that they may liberate themselves from an uncertainty that troubles them and begin a cure immediately. They are persuaded that they are demoniac, but often it is not so. Therefore, in order not to cause misunderstandings with these persons and with those in general whom I do not know, I speak of benedictions rather than exorcisms, and of negativity rather than of possession. Precisely for this reason either I begin with the introductory prayers of the exorcism provided in the *Ritual* or with the *Ritual's* blessing for the sick. If then I am convinced that it is an authentic demonic activity I proceed to the next step.

The Exorcism and Its Origin

Having ascertained that a person may by experiencing the effects of an evil spell, the Church employs a specific instrument to combat it: the exorcism. Here is how the *Catechism* speaks of it: "Exorcism is directed at the expulsion of demons or to the liberation from demonic possession through the spiritual authority which Jesus entrusted to his Church" (no. 1673). In exorcism the Church asks publicly and with authority—the authority that comes from Christ to her—that a person or an object be liberated from the devil's influence. In practice, it is a special prayer of deliverance, reserved to the bishop and to the priests whom he delegates as prescribed by the *Ritual of Exorcisms and Prayers for Particular Circumstances*.[23] During the rite the devil

[23] The official document, the *editio typica* (*De exorcismis et supplicationibus, quibusdam*), was published by decree by the Congregation

is ordered, in the name of Christ, to abandon his influence on the body of the person. In the case of a local exorcism, that is, an exorcism made on a locality, the spirit is ordered to suspend each evil influence on the [place]. It is, however, always the Holy Spirit who liberates.

It is important to note that exorcism is included among the sacramentals, which, according to the *Catechism*, are: "Sacred signs which bear a resemblance to the sacraments. They signify effects, particularly of a spiritual nature, which are obtained through the intercession of the Church. By them men are disposed to receive the chief effects of the sacraments, and various occasions in life are rendered holy" (no. 1667).[24] They are in effect spiritual aids, similar to but not as strong as the seven sacraments and almost extensions of them. Other than exorcisms, sacramentals include: benedictions or blessings; prayers; blessed water, salt, and oil; the Sign of the Cross; sacred images; and many other blessed objects.

Returning to exorcism: the only one authorized to perform an exorcism is an exorcist, that is, a priest delegated by the bishop of

for Divine Worship and the Discipline of the Sacraments, November 22, 1998.

[24] SC 60; cf. CIC, can. 1166; CCEO, can. 867. The *Catechism*'s definition of sacramentals is taken from Vatican II's *Constitution on the Sacred Liturgy*, no. 60. No. 61 adds further clarification: "Thus, for well-disposed members of the faithful, the liturgy of the sacraments and sacramentals sanctifies almost every event in their lives; they are given access to the stream of divine grace which flows from the paschal mystery of the passion, death and resurrection of Christ, the fountain from which all sacraments and sacramentals draw their power. There is hardly any proper use of material things which cannot thus be directed towards the sanctification of men and the praise of God."

the locality, who possesses, by divine mandate, the power to cast out demons and, as such, is the principal exorcist of his diocese. According to the new ritual, the exorcist, who is nominated by the ordinary—that is, by the bishop—must "be knowledgeable, prudent and upright, qualities suitable to the ministry that he is expressively authorized to exercise."

On this point, in order to clarify the discourse, it is appropriate to add some historical notes. It is interesting to observe that, from the beginning, human cultures have been convinced that there exists a god of good and a god of evil and that there are evil forces that lay traps for man to such a point that, in some cases, they take actual possession of him. Therefore, the possession that is known within Christianity is a phenomenology that is known to practically all ancient cultures. Furthermore, we can consider the ancient rituals of protection from evil the precursors of the prayer of exorcism not yet illuminated by the truth of Christ. These concern the early exorcistical practices of the wizards, who were armed with a long oral tradition of ancestral rites, which they used in order to defend themselves from negative forces.

A qualitative leap occurred with the Jewish people when it became clear through divine revelation that only one God exists: Yahweh. The Acts of the Apostles (see 19:13–14), for example, speaks of some itinerant exorcists, sons of the high priest Sceva (and therefore Jewish), who helped themselves to Jesus' name, after having verified that it was more efficacious in casting out demons than their traditional formulas. The fact that exorcists existed at that time is affirmed by Jesus. Having been accused by some Jews of driving out demons in the name of Beelzebub, Jesus asks them: "And if I cast out demons by Beelzebul, by whom do your sons cast them out?" (Luke 11:19). Those sons evidently were Jewish exorcists. Jesus, however, did not avail Himself of the traditional rituals of His people; rather, He drove out demons based solely on the power of His Word. He, in fact, is the great Exorcist of human history.

Jesus, the Son of God before whom the demons give no resistance, then conferred on the twelve apostles, on the seventy-two disciples, on us, and on all believers in Him the power of driving out demons using the power of His name (Matt. 10:1; Luke 10:17; Mark 16:17). There are numerous attestations of the Fathers of the Church in the first three centuries that speak of the disciples of the Lord who cast out demons, placing their hands on the obsessed, without need of particular authorization of the bishop. This mission also had a clear apologetic value since it brought pagans into the Church. Among the more cited exorcists were monks who, thanks to their ascetic life and sanctity, had a great power over the devil. The Institution of the Ministry of Ecclesiastical Exorcism came into existence in the West only after the beginning of the fourth century (the oriental Churches have always considered exorcism a personal charism conferred on each priest who wished to exercise it), and it was immediately placed under the control of the bishops and by some priests delegated by bishops.

Slowly, with the appearance of the Sacramentaries—the official liturgical books of the Church—the first formulas of exorcism began to appear. During the Middle Ages, the awareness of this material increased, and the exorcistical rites were developed and multiplied—often in a disorganized way—and then adapted by the various schools. After 1200 the Church was living a type of contradiction: on one side, an extraordinary theology was developing (St. Thomas Aquinas is of this epoch), and on the other, witches were burning at the stake, mostly poor women who were believed to be incarnated by the devil but, if anything (in the great majority of the cases), were simply possessed by a demon and had need of exorcism.

The rite, which had become too showy, was tidied up and simplified with the Roman Ritual of Paul V (1614), which remained in force up to the promulgation of the *Ritual of Exorcisms and Prayers for Particular Circumstances*, published in 1998. As I have always declared:[25] for more than three centuries, and with serious damage done to those who suffered from spiritual evils, exorcism was practically not practiced; moreover, in the seminaries the subject was practically ignored. The motive, favored by a rationalist mentality, was based on the furious rejection of the witch hunts, the persecutions of heretics, and the religious wars of the past centuries. And so the baby was thrown out with the bath water. Only in the last few years, for various reasons—among which is the growth of the media and their awareness of this material—have things changed a little, but not enough. The situation is much more serious abroad than in Italy.

The *Ritual of Exorcisms and the Prayers for Particular Circumstances*, currently in liturgical use, was the last ritual book to have been revised after Vatican II. When it was published, I criticized it publicly. In particular I contested the fact that in order for an exorcism to be performed, it required the confirmation of clear signs indicating a diabolical possession. This is the problem: in order to ascertain the presence of a possession with a certain margin of security, the best diagnostic instrument is the exorcism itself. In brief, without performing the exorcism, it is difficult to determine if there is truly need of it. My practice of many years tells me this, and I have always maintained it. For this reason, I

[25] See, for example, my *Esorcisti e psichiatri* (Bologna: EDB, 2000), 10.

have continued to use Title XII of the old *Roman Ritual* of 1614, inspired in great part by the prayers written by the theologian Alcuin in the eighth century, entitled *De exorcizandis obsessis a daemonio*, which also grants the exorcism a diagnostic purpose. Naturally I have received authorization from the bishop [to use it]. Since the publication in 2007 of the *motu propio Summorum Pontificum*, however, each priest may freely avail himself of the prayers and benedictions of the old *Rituale Romanum*, and each exorcist may decide whether to avail himself of the new ritual or use the old (that of 1614) in its place. Anyway, after my protests the new ritual was corrected.

How is exorcism regulated in the other Christian churches? With the Orthodox, it is not difficult to find an exorcist. In Romania, for example, each monastery has one. Just knock on the door and ask; it is a little like what happens going to Confession. In other words, the ministry of exorcism has been peacefully reintroduced into the sacrament of Holy Orders.

When People Cannot Find an Exorcist

When people cannot find an exorcist, I advise them to go to a group of the Catholic Charismatic Renewal, who will address prayers of deliverance to them. At times, it can be difficult to find a group of this type near one's residence. In these cases, I proceed with a preliminary discussion with the person and his parents in order to try to understand the symptoms better.

Again, at times I require that the person be seen first by a psychiatrist in order to ascertain that [his problem] does not involve a mental illness. I say this, even though, through experience, I recognize that at times, the symptoms of the two situations—spiritual illness and psychiatric illness—overlap and mingle and that a complete clarification of the nature of the illness is not always reached. Here a simple principle helps: if the cure bears good fruit, one proceeds and intensifies; if one gets nowhere, it is necessary to think of something else. In 1993, I examined this topic with about forty psychiatrists. The question we tried to answer was how to distinguish a psychiatric illness from a spell. I recall saying that the difference becomes clearer if one thinks of a better cure that can be applied to the patient. A psychic illness is cured with natural means, with drugs and with psychological therapy, that is, with human means. But when one has an illness that originates from a spell, the evil can be cured only through supernatural means: prayer, a sacramental life, exorcisms, benedictions, et cetera. At times, it is appropriate to use a combination of the two therapies.

As an indirect consequence, a physical disturbance is sometimes added to a spiritual evil: a tumor, a headache, lacerating pains to the limbs, to the stomach, et cetera. It can happen that these pains, as with vexations, can even have negative diagnoses: from the exams there may be nothing verifiably out of place or no physiological evidence. Then, when the exorcisms resume, these illnesses can also go away. These cases involve diabolical vexations, which at times are also very strong and are probably caused by an evil spell. But the discernment is not always easy. One must proceed case by case and with much prayer.

As for the frequency with which I meet with each person, this cannot be decided presumptively; it depends on each case. Usually I schedule an encounter each month; more often in the more critical cases, if the time and my health permit it. And if the diagnosis is incorrect and there is not any type of spiritual problem? Let us just say that an exorcism does no one any harm.

I am often asked if I am aware of the success—or not—of my prayer. No, I am not. It is only God who acts through prayer.

The exorcist, or the one saying the prayer of liberation, usually is not immediately aware if the person has been liberated. I learn it from the exorcized person some time after the last appointment.

What Happens During an Exorcism?

What happens during the exorcism to the person afflicted by the possession? Above all, it is necessary to say that normally a person affected by possession desires to be liberated from the influence of the demon and as a result will ask to be exorcized. A difficulty can arise, as I have mentioned, in approaching the rite. When the person enters the room where the exorcist works, it sometimes happens that he will begin to feel the influence of the spell more intensely and will manifest a nervousness and discomfort, or, in more serious cases, the person will enter into a trance and must be dragged like a dead weight. In cases like this, there must always be a friend or relative or his pastor with him. At the end of the rite, when I reawaken the person, he will often appear defogged, completely in control again, and will be able to say a prayer peacefully and to exchange a few words with me.

During the rite I ask the unclean spirit his name; each one has a name. When the demon has a biblical name or one given in tradition (for example, Satan, Beelzebub, Lucifer, Zebulun, Meridian, or Asmodeus), we are dealing with "heavyweights" who are much tougher to defeat. Naturally, the Prince of Lies always tries not to respond or is vague, if he does not lie outright. If he does reveal his name, and does not lie, it is because God Himself imposes it on him, which is an anticipatory sign of the liberation. Indeed, the fact that he reveals his name weakens his power significantly and is an encouraging sign. The same can be said when I ask when and how he entered that particular body and when he will leave. But here also it is necessary to be very prudent: rarely does the date [given] correspond to the real date.

Someone asked me if the possession assumes the same extreme forms as [seen in] the famous film *The Exorcist*. Only in part. The film was made with much seriousness, but it is not without exaggeration: most of the time, the cases that exorcists treat are not as serious. This said, there can be extremely violent situations or truly remarkable displays. At times, in the most violent cases (and not only for this are they the most difficult to treat), it happens that the person must be immobilized during the rite in order to impede him from harming himself or others. It is also a good rule to have some of the persons who assist with the prayer intervene to keep the demoniac still.

There can certainly be some very spectacular phenomena during exorcisms, such as speaking in tongues—that is, speaking in foreign or esoteric languages—the overturning of the eyes, and levitation. I recall two cases: the first was that of a young mechanic who worked not far from my community at Rome and who, even before the exorcism was initiated, began to levitate just as I placed my hand on his shoulder. Five people could not hold him still. The second incident was related to me by Father Candido: he exorcized a young peasant girl of seventeen, who was more accustomed to speaking in her dialect than in Italian. While he was reciting the formulas in Latin, Father Candido was distracted by the continuous questions addressed to him by the two priests who had accompanied the girl. After having had enough, he said to them in Greek rather than in Italian (perhaps he was tired), "Shut up! Stop that!" Immediately the girl turned toward him and asked him, in a satanic manner: "Why do you order me to be quiet? Tell it to these two who continue to interrupt you!"

In other cases, the person exorcized can spit nails, glass, or hair. These objects do not come from the esophagus, in which case they would seriously wound the internal organs; rather, they materialize in the vomit coming out of the mouth. Twisted pieces of iron, woven thread, knotted twine, and similar objects can also be found in the cushions and mattresses of the possessed. While interrogating the demon during the prayer, one can sometimes discover the amulet or charm that the wizard was served in order to complete the rite. In all these cases, the objects are burned in order to break the bond. Be aware that it is always necessary to do it with prayer, especially when one finds an indication of the devil invoking the blood of Jesus. Otherwise, as it once happened to Father Candido, when he was still a novice, one risks looking bad because he absorbs the negative effects of it.[26]

[26] "Father Candido and another Passionist priest, both authorized by the bishop, were exorcising a girl. While he was questioning the demon, they discovered that the girl was under a malefice. They asked for its form, and they were told that it was a wooden box, the size of a hand. They asked for the precise location and were told that it was buried three yards deep, near a certain tree. Full of zeal and armed with a spade and a hoe, they went digging on the spot. They found the box, just as they had been told, opened it, and found an obscene figurine among a lot of junk. They sprinkled everything with alcohol and immediately burned everything carefully, until only a pile of ashes remained. But they did not bless the objects before burning them, and they forgot to pray throughout the process, invoking the protection of the blood of Christ. They had repeatedly touched those objects without immediately washing their hands with holy water. The end of the story is this: Father Candido was in bed for three months with a severe stomachache; these pains continued for ten years with less intensity, and they recurred periodically afterward. This was a tough lesson, but it was useful

This last type of phenomenon alone is not enough to certify a diabolical possession, even if there is a good indication. Therefore, it is possible that rather than a possession, there is some vexation. In this case, the exorcist's prudent appraisal will serve to try to establish a reliable diagnosis.

Another question regards the duration of the rite. Here, obviously, it varies from case to case. The battle with Satan is always executed in diverse ways, and one can never tell ahead of time what will happen. We can say that the rite, in the cases in which the possessed does not have violent reactions, lasts, at a minimum, a half hour. In more serious cases, it can go on for hours.

Where is exorcism practiced? According to the new rite of exorcism, whenever possible, the ritual is to be performed in an oratory (a small chapel) or in another appropriate place, with only a few persons present. A crucifix and an image of the Blessed Virgin Mary should be prominent. As for my situation, at times, my congregation, the Society of St. Paul, places some discreet venues in our convent at my disposal. But in thirty years, I must confess that I have alternated between two or three places. The exorcist is considered troublesome or an inconvenience, and it is difficult to find a welcome in places adaptable for him and his work.

The exorcist does not establish a particular formation during the rite: the ritual manual does not specify anything on this matter; one can be to the right, to the left, standing or seated. It is only necessary that he begin with the words "*Ecce crucem Domini*," while he places a strip of his stole on the neck of the presumed demoniac and his right hand on his head.

---

to me and to anyone who may be in the same situation." Amorth, *Esorcisti e psichiatri*, 139.

The final question is difficult to answer: Where does the spirit of evil go once it leaves the person? It is not known: I command him, in the name of Jesus, to return to the eternal inferno or to go under the Cross of Jesus, who is the only one who can order him where to go.

How Many Exorcisms Are Necessary to Achieve Liberation?

How many exorcisms does it require to liberate a demoniac? One can never say beforehand how long it will go forward. Each one is a separate case, and it is not possible to make predictions of the sort. I recall cases that needed only a few encounters and others that I followed for many years. We are in the field of the invisible, so we cannot make precise prognoses. We must place ourselves before the point of view of the divine permission: God permits the devil to persevere against someone for a long time. It is an unfathomable mystery. Why does God permit the evil, and, at times, why does He permit it for such a long time: in order to permit a purification, to grant a greater good to that soul, or as reparation for sins committed by others? A clear understanding eludes us; only many prayers and much faith can help us to accept this mystery.

Is a person always aware that he has been liberated at that precise moment? The liberation and when it happens is established only by God. The way in which it happens is not predictable. In some cases, the person simply becomes aware that the disturbances he was complaining of have passed. In others, and I am referring to more serious cases, the complete cure is often preceded by a worsening of the extraordinary manifestations and a more acute suffering, whose duration varies. But it is the beginning of the end, and it is necessary to be firm in faith and to wait. Here also the book of Francesco Vaiasuso is illuminating: the last period for him was a true nightmare, but at the end, he was rewarded with a complete liberation. At times, one notes an improvement, and then the duration and intensity of the crisis progressively diminishes. This phase involves accustoming oneself to the cure.

How Much Does Faith Matter to the Exorcist?

Faith matters a great deal in the exorcist's work, as it is revealed in a very significant evangelical incident. In the Gospel of Matthew, the apostles are trying to drive a demon out of a boy but are not succeeding. At the request of the boy's father, Jesus comes to their aid and liberates the boy promptly. To the disciples' question as to why their liberation and cure were ineffectual, He responds: "Because of your little faith. For truly, I say to you, if you have faith as a grain of mustard seed, you will say to this mountain, 'Move from hence to yonder place,' and it will move; and nothing will be impossible to you" (Matt. 17:14–21). And in the Gospel of Mark, as we have already seen, He adds: "This kind cannot be driven out by anything but prayer and fasting" (Mark 9:29).

In light of this Gospel passage, a priest who has been appointed by the Church to the ministry of exorcism reduces his effectiveness if he does not adequately cultivate his life of faith. The new ritual also advises prayer and fasting. Therefore, the exorcist is called to a life of a particular sanctity; it is essential to his ministry. The Lord, in His mercy, also takes note of the effort and commitment of the exorcist. I believe that if he puts his all into pursuing a life of sanctity, it is sufficient. It is also important that people pray for him and for the persons he follows. Fortunately, there are many nuns and religious who dedicate themselves to this mission. It is also important to invoke the saints and, among these, especially St. Benedict, the founder of Western monasticism and the patron saint of exorcists. Benedict, a lay monk (and therefore not a priest), had a great capacity for liberating the obsessed thanks to his extraordinary faith. Other important factors are the experience acquired in the field through practice, the sharing of those experiences with colleagues, and continuous study.

To all this I must add that the efficacy of prayer and liberation do not depend solely on the goodwill of the exorcist. For seven years Father Candido Amantini exorcized Angelo Battisti—a close collaborator of Cardinal Agostino Casaroli—without results; Battisti was afflicted by a serious possession that appeared on the day of his retirement. It was another Tuscan exorcist, perhaps less known, Father Angelo Fantoni, who liberated Battisti in just one month. Does it speak poorly of the sanctity of Father Candido? I do not believe so. No one could doubt his faith. Other factors exist that are as important as they are imponderable: God's plans, the spiritual disposition of the possessed, and how much time the spirit had to take root in the person.... Of the cited case, Father Candido explained that there is one who sows the seed and one who gathers, all in accordance with how the Lord arranges it.

Another question often arises: Is the exorcist subject to vexations because of his ministry? In my case, the answer is no. The good God has always spared me from this suffering, and I hope that He will continue to do so. It happens, however, that some of my colleagues have some disturbances—for example, loss of sleep. One can consider these vexations the devil's revenge.

In the work of liberation, can the layman be more efficacious than the exorcist? It happens, certainly. For example, in fourteenth-century Tuscany, when a demoniac could not be liberated, he was sent to St. Catherine of Siena, who, in virtue of her extremely tested faith, often succeeded where the exorcists could not. What matters, as I have said, is faith.

It is more difficult, even if theoretically possible, for people to self-liberate. Jesus said to His disciples: "[I]n my name they will cast out demons" (Mark 16:17). This is valid for liberating not only others, but also oneself. The underlying condition, obviously, is living a life of grace, approaching the sacraments, invoking the help of Mary and the saints, and praying with faith. It is also necessary, however, to say that the spiritually disturbed person does not always manage to live fully this pious desire because of the devil's induced repulsion toward the sacred. In this case, it is necessary to get the help of exorcisms.

Finally, the exorcist may err in making the diagnosis, in particular in discerning between an evil spell and a psychiatric illness. One can always seek verification for a diagnosis by asking for the opinion of another exorcist. But it is not necessary to exaggerate: there are those who go to the exorcist as one goes to the delicatessen, hoping each time to have the diagnosis conform to what he thinks.

The Exorcist's Assistants

As I have already mentioned, the exorcist can be assisted by persons during the rite. As for me, I would have found it very difficult to carry out my ministry if I had had to work without my assistants, but here each one chooses whatever he considers helpful. The presence of qualified persons of proven faith, who are prepared to confront all that can happen during an exorcism, is important for two reasons. Above all, with their presence and their prayers of intercession, they incarnate the living presence of the Church that gathers together and loves her children, especially those who are suffering. The second is the material assistance they give to the person submitting to the exorcism, particularly if he manifests disturbances, such as the impulse to vomit or to react with movements so brusque and violent that he could harm himself and others. Helping to manage the situation physically is part of the task of the assistants.

Here is what the current manual says on the topic: "When an assembly of the faithful, however small, is not present, the exorcist must not forget that already in his person and in that of the faithful tormented by the Evil One, the Church is present. And if some qualified persons are admitted to the exorcism, exhort them to pray intensely for the brother tormented by the demon, both individually and in the forms indicated by the rite."

Those assisting the exorcist must be chosen with judgment: they must live an intense spiritual life, must have firm nerves, must not be easily impressionable, and must be capable of keeping secret the identity of the person possessed and all that is heard during the rite. For instance, it happens sometimes that during an exorcism the spirit will speak. Naturally, most often what the demon relates are lies, or he launches insults and curses. In any case, through all this, it is appropriate for everyone to maintain a respectful silence, including, obviously, the exorcist.

Finally, referring to the assistants, the manual adds: "They must abstain from every form of exorcism, evocative or imperative, which is reserved solely to the exorcist. It is imperative that they do not ever address the spirit, neither directly nor indirectly. They must only think of praying."

Exorcism on a Locality

In the extraordinary action of Satan, local infestation strikes places of residence and common objects of use. The exorcism ritual of 1998 frames the subject like this: "The presence of the devil and of other demons is manifested and concretized not only in the case of persons tempted or possessed, but also when things and places are, in some way, made the object of diabolical action."

At times there are obvious signs that the places and the things of domestic use are infested by Satan: televisions, computers, and lights that turn on and off by themselves; sudden explosions; screams; blows to the walls; shaking ground or shaking beds; stains on sheets and cushions; insect invasions. The examples are so many that it is impossible to enumerate them all. In such cases, one could have the house blessed by a priest, an action that is recommended for any situation. After the priest's benediction, the inhabitants of the house could sprinkle blessed water and salt around the house.

But for extreme evils, one must resort to extreme remedies: the local exorcism. The *Ritual* provides a rite similar to that of an exorcism on a person, with much of the prayer in the imperative form. Each exorcist tries to adapt the prayer to the particular situation. As for me, after having prayed the Lord's Prayer, the Hail Mary, and the Glory Be with the tenants of the house, I personalize the formulas of the ritual of 1614, asking God to liberate the house from the infestations. Then, passing through the individual rooms, I pray repeatedly the first part of the traditional exorcism, which I follow with the aspersion of blessed water. Next, while invoking the intercession of St. Michael the Archangel, I pass through the same area with exorcized incense, blessed with the official formula of the Church. I also use blessed or exorcised salt, placing it in the corners of the rooms, particularly those where the signs of diabolical infestation are more evident.

Exorcisms via the Telephone

The prayer of the exorcism is always personalized. Regarding this, I am frequently asked if it is possible to do exorcisms from a distance; for example, on the telephone or with other means of audio and visual communication that can place the exorcist and the possessed person in contact. My response is yes, even if it is not ordinary. In fact, the rule provided in the *Ritual* is always to meet personally. Physical contact is always preferable in exorcisms; in addition, the sacramentals of oil and blessed water are used on the person and insufflation (the breathing or blowing on the person that symbolizes spiritual influences) is carried out. This obviously cannot happen at a distance. Furthermore, during the exorcism, all the power of the prayer explodes, and often it is necessary that someone hold the obsessed firm, a situation more difficult to create at a distance.

But since many of my patients come from a distance from Rome, where I live, I have, at times, carried out exorcisms via telephone. Obviously I do this only if I know the person and have already ascertained the state of diabolical possession or other spiritual disturbance. But I do not set out to exorcize the first person who picks up the phone.

What effects are obtained? Practically the same as when the person is physically present in the room where I receive him. As the person falls into a trance and the demon begins to speak, I interrogate him and I command him in the name of Jesus to leave the body of the unfortunate one, exactly as I would if the person were in the room with me. Moreover, since the person loses consciousness, I require that someone be at his side to assist him, holding him firm and impeding him from harming himself.

Does the Church authorize exorcisms by telephone? Exorcism is a sacramental, not a sacrament. Sacraments, evidently, cannot be administered at a distance: one cannot hear confessions on the telephone or marry two people by phone. In the case of exorcism, let us say that it is not forbidden: the pastoral duty to assist persons who often are not able to find an exorcist in their area causes me, on rare occasions, to do it on the phone. If all the bishops did their duty, as they should, and appointed at least one exorcist in each diocese, the problem would never be presented.

Finding an Exorcist

How does one find the official exorcist of his diocese? The first thing to do is to call the diocesan office and ask for the information. The office should have the names of the priests on whom this ministry has been conferred. I have been told many times, however, that one risks not receiving concrete answers, especially if there are no exorcists [in the diocese]. In that case, it is necessary to widen your search. And then the long pilgrimages begin, at times at a great distance. One is often forced to make them for years and at great trouble and expense until the liberation is obtained.

Regarding this topic, I would like to remind each bishop that it is his obligation to nominate an exorcist or, as an alternative, to practice the prayers himself, of which he is the primary titular. If the bishop does not perform these duties, indeed, no one else can fill the void, and the result—which my exorcist colleagues and I witness each day—is that the persons who suffer from spiritual evils are forced to experience difficulties and disappointments in their search for an exorcist. What's more, the exorcists, not being numerous, are charged with a workload that is much higher than normal, seeing that they take on persons outside their dioceses. I suffer to think that there are entire nations in which there is not a hint of an exorcist.

Diocesan offices often give evasive responses. In this case, we must resort to the phone tree and check off the names of the exorcists and the places where they receive their patients. With so many braggarts and self-styled liberators in circulation, I sincerely advise that one be certain that the exorcist is a priest appointed by the bishop. It often happens that by exploiting the lack of exorcists, people without scruples and with a great thirst to enrich themselves, promise—obviously behind a high fee—to take away the spell or the evil eye with counter rites. And it concludes with heaping magic on magic, which does nothing but worsen the situation.

And if no exorcist is found? Then one should resort to a Catholic Charismatic Renewal group in his area. Although all may not be equally reliable—this depends principally on who leads them—there remain some that generally, through prayer, can help obtain immediate and concrete benefits.

The International Association of Exorcists

On June 14, 2014, the Congregation for the Clergy (a Vatican committee) approved the statutes for the International Association of Exorcists, which recognized me as the founder and president from 1994 to 2000. I was very content to have assisted from earth, and not from heaven, at the ceremony approving this association, which I had wished for with all my being, together with all the other exorcists, my confreres in the ministry. I was aware during the 1980s that, parallel to the decline of the Faith in our country and in all of Europe, the number of persons going to wizards and getting involved in occultism was increasing exponentially. On the other hand, the exorcists risked acting on their own, without sharing their experiences. I believed that sharing experiences and keeping pace together with theological updates were indispensable.

So, at the beginning of the '90s, I gathered the first group and thus initiated the Italian Association of Exorcists, which has continued to grow. Later, together with the French exorcist René Chenessau and the theologian René Laurentin, we organized the first international convention at Ariccia. We decided then to schedule a similar gathering biennially, and I outlined a statute.

The goal of the association is the formation of a permanent group of exorcists who will meet and share experiences with one another and make known the significance of their ministry within the Church.

I hope that the Church's recognition of this organization will lead to an awareness and an increased sensitivity toward those who are living the drama of an evil spell in solitude and abandonment. I also hope, thanks to this adoption, that more bishops will nominate exorcists in their dioceses, a reality that is still a long way from being accomplished.

Today about 250 members from thirty countries make up the International Association of Exorcists. The majority of these are Italian.

Three Requests for Pope Francis

How do we overcome an endemic lack of exorcists? A bishop once said to me that he did not nominate exorcists because he was afraid of the devil. His confreres could not believe it. It also happens that bishops would like to nominate someone, but they cannot find priests available for this ministry, or, if they are available, they do not carry it out seriously. They counsel those who turn to them to see a psychiatrist, or at best they give them a rapid blessing in order to liberate themselves from the bother. As a result, there are few exorcists, all of them overloaded with work.

How did this happen? I believe that the principal reason is a lack of faith. There are exorcists nominated by their bishops who perhaps do not believe in the existence of the devil, or they are afraid: they believe, but they delude themselves, thinking seriously that if they leave the devil alone, he will not pay any attention to them. Instead, as I have said above, it is precisely the contrary: the more you combat the devil, the more he keeps clear of you!

How does one get around this complex situation, for which the faithful, affected by evil spells, pay the price. If Providence would give me the opportunity, I would go to Pope Francis and share with him three things. First, I would insist that each diocese be obliged to have an exorcist. Second, [I would insist] that seminaries restore the courses in angelology and demonology, and that candidates to the priesthood, in the proximity of their ordination, assist at least one exorcism. Many priests carry out their pastoral ministry without ever having any idea of these spiritual realities, and, as such, they are contributing to the neglect of those who suffer from spiritual evils, especially the young, who have a right to have their needs met. Third, [I would insist] that the ministry of exorcism be extended to all priests without any particular authorization, leaving to each one the liberty to exercise it or not. It seems to me that reserving the exorcistate to the bishops is excessive. What sense is there in preventing priests from carrying out a sacramental when, by virtue of the sacrament of Holy Orders, they have the power to do so much more, such as remitting sins and celebrating the Eucharist, the sacrifice that is the "fount and apex of the whole Christian life"?[27] Why not, instead, leave the liberty of practicing exorcism to each priest if he truly wishes it?

[27] *Lumen Gentium*, no. 11.

6

Other Means of Struggling with the Devil

Prayers of Deliverance and Healing

After exorcism, the most effective means in the struggle against the demon are prayers of deliverance and healing. Initially one can say that these prayers share a similarity with exorcism. Both are pronounced in order to weaken the satanic influence, but with two differences. The first is that exorcism, as the official and public prayer of the Church, directly involves episcopal authority; the prayer of deliverance and healing is a private prayer pronounced on the person by a priest, often the person's pastor, or a layman. It does not involve the official authority of the Church. The second distinction is that the prayer of deliverance is, by nature, a ministry exercised publicly.

Do not be surprised if I speak of laymen. In the Gospel of Mark, before ascending to heaven, Jesus says: "And these signs will accompany those who believe: in my name they will cast out demons" (Mark 16:17). Jesus gave this power first to the twelve apostles and then to the seventy-two disciples. This fact indicates that He intended to extend it to those who believe in Him. This is the scriptural foundation for carrying out prayers of deliverance and healing. Whoever it is, a man, a woman or, with limits, a child, matters little. What matters is faith. The power to drive out demons comes directly from Jesus. No one can deny it or take it away.

Prayers of deliverance, just recently rediscovered in Catholic circles, are very important because, while liberating a person from less-serious evil spells, they also reveal the presence of the extraordinary influence of the demon. Normally they are practiced by groups of the faithful, such as the Catholic Charismatic Renewal, a movement derived from the Pentecostals who initially developed it in the United States and that has, in recent decades, established itself in Italy. The rediscovery of charisms—as, for example, that of speaking in tongues, of healing, of prophecy, and many others—has always been accompanied by the works of liberation. The liberation from the demon, as I said earlier and as I have written many times,[28] is the prior condition for healing some physical illnesses that are tied up with the demon. Once the spiritual liberation has been accomplished, the physical cure is manifested immediately.

Precisely as it happens during the exorcism, at the moment of the invocation of the Holy Spirit and Jesus, the persons affected by evil spirits begin to experience various kinds of suffering. At times, the more organized groups have small nuclei that act on these persons, praying and invoking the powerful liberating action of God. For these prayers to be efficacious, much faith and fasting is necessary. These are without a shadow of a doubt the most efficacious means of defeating Satan.

At times, criticisms are directed at these groups. I have much faith in them. The prayers of healing and deliverance have the same positive effect today that they had in the apostolic Church of two millennia ago. Already in the first Christian communities, as the Acts of the Apostles attest, numerous prodigious cures and

[28] For example, see my book *Esorcisti e psichiatri*, 144–145.

liberations occurred through the works of the first evangelizers, confirming the power of the evangelical announcement of the Resurrection. The Magisterium of the Church explains it like this: "The same New Testament refers to a true and proper concession on the part of Jesus to the Apostles and to the other early evangelizers to heal infirmities.... This power is given in a missionary context, not to exalt their persons, but in order to confirm the mission."[29] His mission, by divine mandate includes the coming of the messianic times through the ministry of healing and liberation.

I spoke earlier of charisms. The Church teaches that "the meaning of charism, is, per se, very broad."[30] A charism, then, is an unmerited gift of the Holy Spirit that a person enjoys for the benefit of the community. A charism is not a trophy, but a task and a service. As to the "charism of healing," St. Paul maintains that it is attributable solely to the liberty of the Spirit, "who apportions to each one individually as he wills" (1 Cor. 12:11). For this, the Magisterium maintains that "in the gatherings of organized prayer that impetrate cures, it would be completely arbitrary to attribute a 'healing charism' to a category of participants; rather they are to trust the very free will of the Holy Spirit who gives a special charism of healing to some in order to manifest the power of grace of the Risen One."[31] It is necessary to instruct the faithful not to divinize the person who carries out this ministry; rather, they must see beyond those who are lent for this service [the exorcist] and focus solely on the Holy Spirit.

Finally, a question: What are the prayers of deliverance? Above all, the Lord's Prayer, when we say "deliver us from the

[29] *Instruction on Prayers for Healing*, no. 1.

[30] Ibid., no. 3.

[31] Ibid., no. 5.

Evil One," which is the exact translation, as the *Catechism of the Catholic Church* affirms (cf. no. 2851). The difference with respect to "deliver us from evil" and "deliver us from the Evil One" is important: the demon has a personal, individual nature [and it must be addressed]. Other prayers using expressions such as "protect me from temptation" or "in the name of Jesus, I command: Satan, go away from here," can also be said. The final part of the *Ritual* lists other formulas that can be of service if necessary.

Mary, Mediatrix of All Graces

"In the end my Immaculate Heart will triumph": Mary's prophecy at Fátima reassures us that besides the body-to-body [struggle] with the demon (the exorcism), the earthly anticipation of the eschatological struggle between the Mother of God and the ancient dragon (cf. Rev. 12) also has her attention. Despite rampant sin and despite the man who abandons God, considering him only a useless impediment to his own unrestrained liberty, the tribulations of the Church will have an end. And the finale will be good: God will have the last word on history. For this reason, Mary is always invoked during the exorcism; although, to tell the truth, the old ritual did not include an invocation to her. Adding her to the ceremony is a practice I borrowed from Father Candido, however. It is a necessity, and the current ritual has gotten around this deficiency. During the prayer, the priest repeatedly invokes her intercession and her powerful action. Without her, little is accomplished in the struggle against Satan. It is always God who liberates one from his influence — it is good to keep repeating it — but His ear is especially attuned to the mediation of Mary, the Mother of His Son.

What role does the Virgin have in the liberation of the obsessed? Mary, as the Hail Mary says, is "full of grace." She is the mediatrix of God's every grace for all men, particularly for those who suffer much, including those who suffer from spiritual evils. The enmity between Mary and Satan—proclaimed solemnly by God in the first book of Genesis (Gen. 1:3–15) and manifest in the eschatological struggle with the dragon—makes her the number-one enemy of the demon. She will be the one to crush his head at the end of time.

The help of the Virgin, however, goes beyond the exceptional situations of the demoniacs. In man's every struggle against Satan and sin, it is always she who represents the extraordinary and the irreplaceable. The demon is terrified of her. In order to be very clear, I wish to cite an episode at which I personally assisted many years ago. During an exorcism, Father Candido asked the devil a question: "Why are you more afraid when I invoke Mary than when I implore God Himself?" He responded: "I feel more humiliated being conquered by a simple creature than by God Himself."

Mary is a creature like us, but, having been elevated to be the Mother of God, she has extraordinary power. Also for this reason I ask the persons who assist me to pray the Rosary. It is the most advisable prayer in that context, prayed individually, not aloud and collectively, as it is often prayed in church before Mass, so as not to disturb the exorcism. I would add that the Rosary, being the prayer most appreciated by our Lady, is an extremely powerful arm against the devil, and I warmly recommend it to anyone suffering from spiritual evils. This prayer has, in fact, a strong power of protection and liberation from evil. One day Sister Lucia, a seer of Fátima, revealed that God has conferred a power so great on the Rosary that there is no evil—personal, family, or social—that cannot be defeated by its recitation with faith.

What, then, can we ask of Mary in the Rosary? There is nothing else to ask of her except for the gift of peace—for the world certainly, but also for ourselves; for the serenity of our heart, so that we may be able to accept our crosses, so that we may know how to recognize the gifts that we receive each day from the good God and thank Him for this. It is also important to pray the Rosary together as a family in order to invoke peace in our homes and in our parochial communities, in workplaces, in nations, and in the world. Wars and the division of souls are unequivocal signs of the presence of the devil, which, not by chance, in Greek means "divider."

I also recall that on March 25, 1984, St. John Paul II consecrated the world to Mary. It was a very important gesture in an epoch in which communism still represented an explicit threat to Christianity. During an exorcism, I asked an unclean spirit who was persecuting someone why he had so much hatred toward John Paul II. He replied: "Because he has ruined our plans." I imagine that he was referring to the fall of communism. At Fátima, when the Virgin affirmed that her "Immaculate Heart will triumph," what could it mean if not to trust in the Lord and her maternal help always—particularly before the danger of discouragement that lies in wait for everyone, but, above all, for those suffering from evil spirits, because often waiting for the results can seem interminable. It also means that, with the help of Mary, we must continuously engage ourselves in converting to God, so that we will know how to do His will—that is, to pardon and to love—and so that we may know how to make every event an occasion of sanctification and the realization of God's plan for us. Mary brings us to Jesus, because initially she allowed the Holy Spirit to touch her intimately, permitting her to generate Jesus in time.

The Intercession of the Saints

The saints in heaven intercede for us with great power and efficacy. We must pray to them often. As we profess in the Creed, with them and with the suffering souls in purgatory we are building up what we call the community of saints. It is worth the trouble to read what Vatican II has declared regarding this subject: "Until the Lord shall come in His majesty, and all the angels with Him [cf. Matt. 25:31] and death being destroyed, all things are subject to Him [cf. 1 Cor. 15:26–27], . . . all in various ways and degrees are in communion in the same charity of God and neighbor and all sing the same hymn of glory to our God. For all who are in Christ, having His Spirit, form one Church and cleave together in Him [cf. Eph. 4:16]."[32]

Here is an important motive for hoping to win the struggle against the devil but also to overcome the anguish and suffering that entangles us at times. With those who already enjoy the vision of God in paradise, an intense exchange of spiritual benefits takes place. Because of their more intimate union with Christ, the inhabitants of heaven do not cease to intercede for us with the Father, offering Him the merits that they acquired on earth through Jesus Christ. Thus, our weakness is greatly helped by their fraternal solicitude.[33]

For the one who is troubled by a demon, the invocation of the saints during the rite of exorcism manifests this trust of the Church in their presence. But apart from this, I counsel, in personal prayer, the frequent recitation of the litanies of the saints, choosing one's own patron or those to whom one is particularly devoted. Their presence is also mediated through devotion and

[32] *Lumen Gentium*, no. 49.

[33] Ibid.

through the use of their relics, which disturb many demonic actions. As I outlined not long ago, it is necessary to remember that the souls in purgatory can also intercede for us and are also called upon for liberation from the influences of the demon. To offer one's spiritual sufferings in order to shorten their purification is another meritorious work.

Which particular saints should those who suffer from spiritual evils call upon? I advise invoking those saints who have experienced the same disturbances; for example, Blessed Eustace (in the secular life, Lucrezia Bellini), a Benedictine nun from Padua who lived in the fifteenth century. She died at the age of twenty-five after having been possessed by a demon from the age of four. Her religious life, begun at eighteen, was also heavily conditioned by that grave possession, which she tolerated, offering her sufferings to expiate the sins of those who caused her tribulations. Even her own consecrated sisters mistreated her, annoyed by the disturbances her possession caused the communal life of their convent. Only shortly before her death did they understand that they had been living with a saint. Even today many pray before her tomb in the church of St. Peter, imploring the grace of liberation.

As for me, when I practice exorcisms, I feel the very powerful presence of St. Pio of Pietrelcina, St. Catherine of Bologna, and St. John Paul II. Of this last, I know for certain that he personally practiced at least three exorcisms in his private chapel in the Vatican. When I pronounce his name, the demons are literally infuriated.

I have been asked if, during the exorcism, the demon will pronounce the name of the saint. Normally he does not. It can happen that demons will make a reference to God, to the Virgin, and to some saints, although they have an authentic terror of them, but it never happens that they are able to use their names directly; if they must mention them, they use substitutions. Jesus is referred to in reference to the priest who is performing the exorcism, such as, "your leader" or "your superior"; our Lady is "that one there" or "the thief of souls"; the saints are "assassins." They oppose [the saints] because, by their prayers, [the saints] steal souls from [the demons'] claws. This is in confirmation of all that we have said.

The Help of the Angels

What role do the angels have? We have already spoken of their choice for or against God in the third chapter. The word *angel* derives from the Greek *angelos* and means "messenger of God." The angels are spiritual creatures, without matter. They are pure forms and have a nature different from that of men, who have a material and spiritual nature together. The angels are subdivided into angelic hierarchies according to the mission that is entrusted to them by God. They cannot reproduce or die: in fact, they have been created directly by God.

At the moment of our birth, Divine Providence assigns each of us a guardian angel, with the specific task of protecting us, assisting us, and interceding for us so that at the end of life we can arrive at our destination, which is paradise.

We have already seen that entire legions of angels have chosen the tragic road of rebellion against God, refusing to obey and to adore Him and, indeed, they tried to substitute themselves for Him. As a consequence of their choice, the devils radically changed their mission: now, in fact, they use their superfine intelligence for the unique objective of destroying men and making them their companions in misfortune. As Revelation tells us, that gigantic war that was fought in the heavens among the angels and the demons has another battlefield here on earth: they are in a continuous battle for our lives and our hearts.

From all this, one can affirm that the angels who remained faithful to God have a certain degree of power against ordinary temptations as well as extraordinary spiritual evils. Why? Because they are of the same nature as the devils, and they fight with the same spiritual arms. The angels intercede with God in favor of the one being tempted; for this reason, we exorcists always invoke them during the prayers on the obsessed. Among the angels we give precedence to the three archangels, in particular to St. Michael, the most powerful in the struggle against demons. Incidentally, I am among those who regret that, after Vatican II, the prayer of protection to St. Michael the Archangel, recited after Mass, was eliminated. It seems to me to have created an impoverishment, a void. It is true, however, that one can freely say it privately.

In brief, it is good to invoke the angels often, even apart from their help with extraordinary spiritual evils. I always advise imploring their assistance. Our guardian angels have a special power of intercession with God, which is always the beginning of liberations (from demons). The angels help, they intercede, but they themselves do not have the power to liberate the possessed from the terrible effects of demons.

Sacred Objects and Blessings

One can also use blessed objects in the struggle against Satan. This practice is advisable for everyone, not only for those with specific spiritual problems. It is always appropriate to keep sacred images, statues, or blessed niches in the home; sacred objects are a sign of our fidelity and belonging to God. They constitute a protection from the Evil One because they are a constant reminder of our consecration to the Trinity in baptism. But they are also important because they are a form of visible testimony toward those who live with us and those who visit us in our home.

It is also a good thing to keep some blessed objects with you in a purse or a backpack or in a briefcase. Those that come to mind are the St. Benedict medal, which is placed in crucifixes, and the Miraculous Medal, presented to St. Catherine Labouré in 1830, on which Mary is configured with the inscription: "O, Mary conceived without sin, pray for us who have recourse to you." On the other side there is a large M, which signifies Mary, and two hearts—those of Jesus and Mary—that signify (as would be revealed in 1917 at Fátima) that it is the will of God that Mary and her Son be prayed to together.

We can also cite other objects: scapulars and the images of the saints and their relics. It is necessary to specify that these objects have no value if they are not sustained by a concrete faith, based on charity. They must not be a means of indulging in superstitions or carried as a talisman or good-luck piece, which would be falling into a magical attitude, something that is gravely contrary to faith. Pope Francis confirms all this in the encyclical *Evangelii Gaudium* (*The Joy of the Gospel*), which encourages everyone to seek a "renewed personal encounter with Jesus Christ each day.... I ask all of you to do this unfailingly."[34] This is the Faith, the personal encounter with Jesus, the only one who can change our lives and liberate us from our egoism.

Let us return to the blessed objects. There is a passage in the Bible that confirms their importance: "And God did extraordinary miracles by the hands of Paul, so that handkerchiefs or aprons were carried away from his body to the sick, and diseases

[34] *Evangelii Gaudium*, no. 3.

left them and the evil spirits came out of them" (Acts 19:11–12). My exorcistical experience confirms that demons have a natural repulsion toward all sacred objects but also toward the instruments of daily life that have been blessed—automobiles, utensils, et cetera—because, as such, they extract all or part of their power. For this reason, also it is a good rule to have them blessed.

Usually, whoever has been affected by an evil spell immediately perceives that an object has been blessed. On this subject, a case was made known to me of a mother who suffered much from the furious attitudes and cursing of her son, a young man who was a mechanic by profession. This behavior began suddenly in the life of the youth: he grew up serene in a sane family and never displayed any particular anxiety, much less violence. One day the mother had some of his casual clothing blessed. When he returned from work, after taking a shower, he put on those clothes. It took only a few seconds for him to take them off in a hurry, nearly ripping them off, and put on his dirty overalls. Well, he never again put on those clothes, and he always kept them separate from the unblessed clothes in his closet. Evidently that young man had need of an exorcism.

Can these objects be blessed preventively? Yes, certainly. Here also, the sense of the benediction is not that of conferring a magical protection or a super power on an object. Rather, it is a prayer of supplication pronounced by the priest, asking God to increase grace in our daily life and to obtain the protection and the intercession of the person represented or invoked in the object. I am always taken aback when, in automobiles, in public localities, and in private houses, I see a sacred image and a superstitious object, a horseshoe or something similar, close together. What does one have to do with the other?

I recall a case that I related many years ago on Radio Maria. I was called to bless a house because the persons living in it felt strange presences there. Once I entered, I did not see any sacred images on the walls. Rather, hanging on the door was an enormous red "horn" [an object employed to keep away the "evil eye"] . . . and I reprimanded the persons who had invited me. "How," I said, "can you seek protection from evil and [at the same time] hang amulets on your door? Don't you know that, as signs of superstition, these are evil objects?"

In conclusion, having objects and persons blessed by priests, but without ceding to superstition, is appropriate. For this reason, I always invite my priestly confreres to bless the objects of the faithful whenever they request it.

Blessed Salt, Water, and Oil: Allies in the Struggle against the Evil One

Salt, oil, and water blessed or exorcized according to the regulations of the Benedictional are sacramentals.[35] They are useful instruments if their action is sustained by faith. Exorcists often avail themselves of them. Blessed water, moreover, in substitution of the penitential act, can be used in the Eucharistic celebration to sprinkle the people.

Who can bless and exorcize these elements? Any priest who recites the prescribed prayers of the Benedictional can exorcize and bless water, salt, and oil. In the prayer of benediction, one prays to God because, through the aspersion with the blessed

[35] The Benedictional is a book of benedictions and blessings collected from those in the Sacramentary (that part of the Missal containing the prayers and directions for the Mass and a number of sacramental formulas).

water, one obtains pardon for sins, the defense from the Evil One, and the gift of divine protection. The prayer of exorcism together with the water eradicates the power of the demon and chases him away. In fact, how could the devil and holy water get along?

The blessed oil, applied to a person, has the same protective effect. I use it and find it very efficacious with the demoniacs who have submitted to evil spells through ingesting food or cursed beverages. These persons often manifest external signs such as stomachaches, sobbing, and wheezing while they are in a situation of spiritual stress—that is, during the exorcism, during Mass, while praying, and so forth. The cure in these cases is manifested concretely with the expulsion of the objects or organic substances that have incorporated the spell. The anointing with blessed oil and the ingestion of blessed water are very useful in these difficult situations. The blessed salt is used, above all, to protect the localities—houses, stalls, et cetera—from the influence of the Evil One. Usually, as we have already explained, it is placed on the threshold of the house and in the corners of the individual rooms that are reputed to be infested.

7

The Principles of Christian Eschatology: Death, Judgment, Heaven, Purgatory, Hell

Heaven, the Kingdom of Love

I wish to conclude this book with some basic notions of Christian eschatology,[36] which, because of the Resurrection of Christ give a reason for great hope to everyone — in particular, to those who suffer from evil spells. Our life, our earthly pilgrimage, and our suffering are not the fruit of a blind randomness; rather, they are ordered for our greater good and definitive friendship with God.

Let us begin, then, precisely from paradise, the final goal and the reason for which we have been created. "Those who die in God's grace and friendship and are perfectly purified live for ever with Christ. They are like God for ever, for they 'see him as he is,' face to face [1 John 3:2; cf. 1 Cor. 13:12; Rev. 22:4]" (CCC, no. 1023). Our Faith guarantees that in paradise we shall enjoy the vision of God; that is, we shall become participants in that same happiness that the divine Persons enjoy among themselves: "The life of the blessed consists in the full and perfect possession

[36] The branch of theology that deals with the four last things: death, judgment, heaven, and hell.

of the fruits of the redemption accomplished by Christ. He makes partners in his heavenly glorification those who have believed in him and remained faithful to his will. Heaven is the blessed community of all who are perfectly incorporated into Christ" (CCC, no. 1026).

Will we be modified? Will we always be ourselves? What of our identity? The elect—those who rise to paradise—will live in God but always conserving their true and definitive identity, that is, their own name. The *Catechism* clarifies that paradise surpasses our every capacity to understand and indicates that the Bible describes it with many simple and intuitive images: "life," "light," "peace," a "wedding banquet" and the "heavenly Jerusalem" (see CCC, no. 1027). These are simple human experiences used as analogies, but they give us only a pallid image of what eternal life shall be. In fact, when we speak of it, we are able only to stammer and stutter.

Regarding the condition of the blessed, we can say very little: revelation speaks, as I have said, only through allusions and metaphors. Let us consider St. Peter and his experience in the episode of the Transfiguration (Matt. 17:1–8; Mark 9:2–8; Luke 9:28–36), of which he never speaks in his letters; or St. Paul, when he relates having been "caught up to the third heaven" (2 Cor. 12:2), but then he does not enter into details; he makes us understand only that it is a state of perfect beatitude (2 Cor. 12:4: "he heard things that cannot be told, which man may not utter"). What we do know is that our dear deceased, who by now live in God, see us from on high and follow us with love; and they are always near to us, interceding in our favor. When, out of divine mercy, we shall join them in the other life, we shall certainly recognize them, but our rapport with them will be different, because this will occur in God, in the total fullness of His love.

A question arises spontaneously: What need did the Trinity have for creatures, for men and angels, when It was already perfect and absolutely sufficient in Itself? The Trinity did it solely out of love, gratuitous and unconditional love for us. The advantage is solely ours: love, joy, and happiness, for all, in paradise.

There are degrees of participation in the joy and love of God. This degree of rank is given according to the level of sanctity each person has reached during his lifetime: the joy of St. Francis of Assisi, for example, will be different from that of the good thief. There is a difference between men on earth, and there will be a difference in paradise. It is similar to what happens with the stars in heaven: there are those that shine brighter and those that shine a little less. So also it will be with men in the glorious resurrection: all of us shall be resplendent, but each one with a different proportion. Each one will have that maximum of splendor and happiness that he is personally capable of, based on how he has lived his life. Some will have a greater capacity and others less, but without envy or jealousy toward each other. Indeed, each one will know complete joy. A verse from Dante's *Divine Comedy* comes to mind: "In his will is our peace."[37] In paradise there is no jealousy; each one is in the will of God, and in His will there is peace. Eternal peace is definitive, where each tear, each sorrow, and all envy will be wiped away.

The Souls in Purgatory

Purgatory is the place, or, better, the state to which come the souls that have need of a purification and therefore have not been immediately admitted to contemplate the face of God. This purification is necessary in order to arrive at sanctity, the condition that heaven requires. The *Catechism* speaks of the souls in

[37] Dante, *Paradiso*, canto 3, line 85.

purgatory: "All who die in God's grace and friendship, but still imperfectly purified, are indeed assured of their eternal salvation; but after death they undergo purification, so as to achieve the holiness necessary to enter the joy of heaven" (no. 1030). We can understand that there are gradations or diverse states in purgatory; each one accomodates the situation of the soul that arrives there. There are the lower strata, more terrible because they are closer to hell, and the more elevated that are less terrible because they are much closer to the happiness of paradise. The level of purification is linked to this state.

The souls in purgatory are in a state of great suffering. We know, in fact, that they can pray for us and that they can obtain many graces for us, but they can no longer merit anything for themselves. The time for meriting graces finishes with death. Purged souls can, however, receive our help in order to abbreviate their period of purification. This occurs in a powerful way through our prayers, with the offering of our sufferings, paying attention at Mass, specifically at funerals or at Gregorian Masses, celebrated for thirty consecutive days. This last practice was introduced by St. Gregory the Great in the sixth century, ispired by a vision he had of a confrere who died without confessing himself and, having gone to purgatory, appeared to him, asking him to celebrate some Masses in his favor. The pope celebrated them for thirty days. At that point, the deceased appeared to him again, happy for having been admitted to paradise. One must take care: this does not mean that it will always work this way: that would be a magical attitude, unacceptable and erroneous toward a sacrament. In fact, it is solely God who decides these matters when He wills it through His divine mercy.

On the subject of Masses, it is necessary to say that they can be applied to a particular deceased, but, at the last moment, it is God who destines them to those who have a real need. For example, I often celebrate Masses for my parents, whom I believe in my conscience are already in paradise. Only God in His mercy will destine the benefits of my Masses to those who have more need, each one according to the criteria of justice and goodness reached during his life.

Regarding all that I have said, I wish warmly to advise that it is better to expiate suffering in this life and become a saint than, in a minimalist way, to aspire to purgatory, where the pains are long-lasting and heavy.

The Pains of Hell

The book of Revelation says that "the great dragon was thrown down, that ancient serpent, who is called the Devil and Satan, the deceiver of the whole world—he was thrown down to the earth, and his angels were thrown down with him" (Rev. 12:9). Why were they hurled down to the earth? Because the punishment they were given is that of persecuting men, trying to lead them to eternal hell, rendering them their unfortunate companions for an eternity of suffering and torment. How can this drama, which involves everyone, enter into the plans of God? As we have said, the next reason is the liberty granted by God to His creatures. Certainly we know that the mission of Satan and his acolytes is to ruin man, to seduce him, to lead him toward sin, and to distance him from the full participation in divine life, to which we have all been called, which is paradise.

Then there is hell, the state in which the demons and the condemned are distanced from the Creator, the angels, and the saints in a permanent and eternal condition of damnation. Hell, after all, is self-exclusion from communion with God. As the *Catechism* states: "We cannot be united with God unless we freely choose to love him. But we cannot love God if we sin gravely against him, against our neighbor or against ourselves" (no. 1033). The one who dies in mortal sin without repenting goes to hell; in an impenitent way, he has not loved. It is not God who predestines a soul to hell; the soul chooses it with the way [the person] has lived his life.

We have some stories about hell that, because they are taken from private revelations or experiences, do not bind the faithful, but, nevertheless, have a notable value. I have spoken on more occasions in my books and in my interviews of the experience of St. Faustina Kowalska, who in her diary writes of her spiritual journey to hell:

> Today I was led by an angel to the chasms of hell. It is a place of great torture; how awesomely large and extensive it is! I saw many kinds of tortures: the first torture that constitutes hell is the loss of God; the second is perpetual remorse of conscience; the third is that one's condition will never change; the fourth is the fire that will penetrate the soul without destroying it—a terrible suffering, since it is purely a spiritual fire, lit by God's anger; the fifth torture is a continual darkness and a terrible suffocating smell, and, despite the darkness, the devils and the souls of the damned see each other and all the evil, both of others and their own; the sixth torture is the constant company of Satan; the seventh is horrible despair, hatred of God, vile words, curses and blasphemies. These are the tortures suffered by all the damned together, but that is not the end of sufferings. There are special tortures destined for particular souls. These are the torments of the senses. Each soul undergoes terrible and indescribable sufferings, related to the manner in which it has sinned.

> There are caverns and pits of torture where one form of agony differs from another....
>
> Let the sinner know that in the same way that he sinned he will be tortured throughout all eternity.... What I have written is a pale shadow of the things I saw. But I noticed one common element: that most of the souls in hell are those who disbelieved there is a hell. Consequently, I pray even more fervently for the conversion of sinners. I incessantly plead for God's mercy upon them.

It is shocking.

I also wish to recall the testimony of Gloria Polo, a dentist from Colombia, who lived an extraordinary experience that literally agitated her life. On May 5, 1995, this lady was struck by lightning, which nearly charred her body. Gloria was a lukewarm Catholic, critical of the Church, a supporter of euthanasia, very dedicated to the care of her body and interested in the New Age. She did not disdain frequenting sorcerers and fortune-tellers in order to have them predict her future. After she was struck by lightning, her body remained lifeless for several minutes, in cardiac arrest.

During that time Gloria had a near-death experience: she found herself in a tunnel with a bright light at the end, in which she met her deceased parents: it was paradise. But, at the same time, she had strong feelings of guilt for the slight faith she had practiced during her life that was impeding her from remaining in that light. She then fell into a deep abyss. Many demons began to run after her, trying to capture her. She related how she had to run through many tunnels that kept getting lower and lower and were organized like beehives filled with people who were crying and gnashing their teeth with terrifying screams. Some of these were suicides. Gloria was convinced that she found herself in a place of spiritual death and eternal condemnation, with no return and no hope. It was hell. Only the intervention of St. Michael the Archangel, who had grabbed her by the feet and brought her back up, prevented her from precipitating definitively. Here is how she speaks of it today: "It was a terrible and truly painful moment. When I arrived there, the light that still remained in my spirit bothered those demons; all the horrifying unclean beings that live there immediately began attacking me.... Brothers and sisters, they are living a gloom and hatred that burns and devours and lays bare. There are no words to describe that horror!"[38]

Stories and visions like those just described, although in a concise form, have to make us reflect. For this reason Our Lady of Fátima said to the seers: "Pray and offer sacrifices; too many souls go to hell because there is no one to pray and offer sacrifices for them."

Being in the kingdom of hate, damned souls are subjected to the torment of the demons and to the sufferings they reciprocally inflict on one another. As I have said above, in the course of my exorcisms, I have understood that there is a hierarchy of demons, just as there is with angels. More than once I have found myself involved with demons who were possessing a person and who demonstrated a terror toward their leaders. One day, after having done many exorcisms on a poor woman, I asked the minor demon who was possessing her: "Why don't you go away?" And he replied: "Because if I go away from here, my leader, Satan,

[38] To read the complete story, see Irene Corona, *Gloria Polo, Da sostenitrice dell'eutanasia a paladina della vita* (Feletto Umberto: Edizioni Segno, 2012).

will punish me." There exists in hell a subjugation dictated by terror and hatred. This is the abysmal contrast with paradise, the place where everyone loves one another and where, if a soul sees someone holier, that soul is immensely happy because of the benefit it receives from the happiness of another.

Some say that hell is empty. The response to this affirmation is found in chapter 25 of Matthew's Gospel, where it speaks of the Last Judgment: the upright will go to eternal life and the others, the cursed, will go to the eternal fire. We can certainly hope that hell is empty, because God does not wish the death of a sinner but that he convert and live (see Ezek. 33:11). For this He offers His mercy and saving grace to each one. In the Gospel of John Jesus says: "If you forgive the sins of any, they are forgiven; if you retain the sins of any, they are retained" (John 20:23); thus He insists on our continuous conversion supported by the grace of the sacraments, in particular the sacrament of Penance.

Returning to the question of hell, whether it is empty or not: unfortunately, I fear that many souls go there, all those who persevere in their choice of distancing themselves from God to the end. Let us meditate often on this. Pascal said it well: "Meditation on hell has filled paradise with saints."

The Judgment on Life

The *Catechism* speaks of the particular judgment: "The New Testament speaks of judgment primarily in its aspect of the final encounter with Christ in his second coming, but also repeatedly affirms that each will be rewarded immediately after death in accordance with his works and faith" (no. 1021). And further on it adds: "Each man receives his eternal retribution in his immortal soul at the very moment of his death, in a particular judgment that refers his life to Christ: either entrance into the blessedness of heaven—through a purification[39] or immediately[40]—or immediate and everlasting damnation" (no. 1022). Then it adds the criterion with which this judgment will occur, taken from the writings of St. John of the Cross: "At the evening of life, we shall be judged on our love."[41]

The first thing that I would emphasize is precisely this last: the final criterion of our judgment will be the love that we have had toward God and toward our brothers and sisters. How, then, will this particular judgment occur? At times, I run into persons who are convinced that immediately after death they will meet Jesus in person and that He will give them a piece of His mind for some of their dolorous affairs. Frankly, I do not think that it will happen like this. Rather, I believe that, immediately after death, each of us will appear before Jesus, but it will not be the Lord who will review our lives and examine the good and the bad each of us has done. We ourselves shall do it, in truth and honesty. Each one will have before himself the complete vision of his life, and he will immediately see the real spiritual state of his soul and will go where his situation will bring him. It will be a solemn moment of self-truth, a tremendous and definitive moment, as definitive as the place where we shall be sent. Let us consider the case of the person who goes to purgatory. It will involve the sorrow of not immediately going to paradise that will make him understand that his purification on earth was not complete, and he will feel the immediate need of purifying himself. His desire of acceding to the vision of God will be strong, and the desire

[39] Cf. Council of Lyons II (1274): DS 857–858; Council of Florence (1439): DS 1304–1306; Council of Trent (1563): DS 1820.

[40] Cf. Benedict XII, *Benedictus Deus* (1336): DS 1000–1001; John XXII, *Ne super his* (1334): DS 990.

[41] St. John of the Cross, *Dichos* 64.

for liberation from the weight of the pains accumulated during his earthly life will be compelling.

The Last Judgment: It Will Be Love That Will Judge Us

Let us end with the universal judgment:

> The Last Judgment will come when Christ returns in glory. Only the Father knows the day and the hour; only he determines the moment of its coming. Then through his Son Jesus Christ he will pronounce the final word on all history. We shall know the ultimate meaning of the whole work of creation and of the entire economy of salvation and understand the marvelous ways by which his Providence led everything towards its final end. (CCC, no. 1040)

This is one of the most difficult realities to understand. The Last Judgment coincides with the return of Christ; however we do not know the precise time it will occur. We know that it will be preceded immediately by the resurrection of the dead. In that precise moment, the history of the world will definitively and globally end. The *Catechism* again specifies: "In the presence of Christ, who is Truth itself, the truth of each man's relationship with God will be laid bare [cf. John 12:49]" (no. 1039).

The essential question is: What is the concrete rapport that each man has with God? As I have mentioned, the solemn response is found in the Gospel of Mathew. The saved and the damned will be chosen on the basis of their recognition or rejection of Christ in the infirm, in the hungry, and in the poor (Matt. 25:31–46). Two essential elements emerge from this. The first is a division, a schism, between those going to paradise and those going to hell, between the saved and the condemned. The second regards the manner in which this judgment will be accomplished—with love. God's Commandments and every other precept are summarized solely in one commandment: "[L]ove one another as I have loved you" (John 15:12).

We can easily understand that this command is addressed to each human conscience in every age, including those who lived before Christ and those, who today, as in centuries past, never heard anyone speak of the Son of Man. Therefore, the finale of this stupendous passage is the beautiful passage from Mathew: "Truly, I say to you, as you did it to one of the least of these my brethren, you did it to me" (Matt. 25:40).

If each man—apart from his religion, his culture, his epoch, and any other circumstance—has loved his neighbor, he has also loved the Lord Jesus in person. Any rapport with our brothers and sisters in any locality, any age, or any situation is, all in all, a rapport with Jesus Christ in person. Each human creature who achieves fulfillment in his human relationships is, at the same time, relating to God. For this reason, the love of neighbor is the fundamental precept of life. John the Evangelist helps us to understand that we cannot say that we love God, whom we cannot see, if we do not love our brother, whom we can see (cf. 1 John 4:20). The love that will judge us will be the same [love] that we have (or have not) practiced toward others, the same [love] that Jesus lived in His earthly experience and taught us in the Gospels, the same [love] to which we are entitled through the sacraments, through prayer, and through a life of faith. The ability to love comes from grace, and it is much reduced in those who do not know Christ; and even more so in those who know Him but do not follow Him, a choice that assumes a serious sin. Indeed, Jesus said: "He who believes and is baptized will be saved; but he who does not believe will be condemned" (Mark 16:16).

On the other hand, in announcing the extraordinary Jubilee of Mercy, Pope Francis reminds us that the other fundamental aspect of the question is that the love with which we shall be judged will be the Love of mercy. "Mercy is the ultimate and supreme act by which God comes to meet us."[42] This mercy, he says, "is the bridge that connects God and man and opens our hearts to the hope of being loved forever despite our sinfulness." God's compassionate glance and His desire to live in total communion with us opens our hearts to the hope that each sin and each failure inflicted on man by his great enemy, Satan, will be looked upon with the eyes of a loving and accepting Father. Therefore, let us live full of hope, because we know that, even in the difficulties of our life's journey, God will wipe away all the tears from our eyes. On that day "death shall be no more, neither shall there be mourning nor crying nor pain any more, for the former things have passed away" (Rev. 21:4).

[42] Cf. *Misericordiae Vultus*, no. 2.

Prayer for Deliverance (approved for the laity)

My Lord, You are all powerful, You are God,
You are Father.
We beg You through the intercession and help
Of the Archangels Michael, Raphael, and Gabriel
for the deliverance of our brothers and sisters
who are enslaved by the Evil One.
All saints of heaven, come to our aid.

From anxiety, sadness, and obsessions,
We beg You, free us, O Lord.
From hatred, fornication, envy,
We beg You, free us, O Lord.
From thoughts of jealousy, rage, and death,
We beg You, free us, O Lord.
From every thought of suicide and abortion,
We beg You, free us, O Lord.
From every form of sinful sexuality,
We beg You, free us, O Lord.
From every division in our family, and every harmful friendship,
We beg You, free us, O Lord.
From every sort of evil spell, malefice, witchcraft, and every form of occult,
We beg You, free us, O Lord.

Lord, You who said, "I leave you peace, my peace I give you," grant that, through the intercession of the Virgin Mary, we may be liberated from every evil spell and enjoy Your peace always. In the name of Christ, our Lord. Amen.

Sophia Institute

Sophia Institute is a nonprofit institution that seeks to nurture the spiritual, moral, and cultural life of souls and to spread the Gospel of Christ in conformity with the authentic teachings of the Roman Catholic Church.

Sophia Institute Press fulfills this mission by offering translations, reprints, and new publications that afford readers a rich source of the enduring wisdom of mankind.

Sophia Institute also operates two popular online Catholic resources: CrisisMagazine.com and CatholicExchange.com.

Crisis Magazine provides insightful cultural analysis that arms readers with the arguments necessary for navigating the ideological and theological minefields of the day. *Catholic Exchange* provides world news from a Catholic perspective as well as daily devotionals and articles that will help you to grow in holiness and live a life consistent with the teachings of the Church.

In 2013, Sophia Institute launched Sophia Institute for Teachers to renew and rebuild Catholic culture through service to Catholic education. With the goal of nurturing the spiritual, moral, and cultural life of souls, and an abiding respect for the role and work of teachers, we strive to provide materials and programs that are at once enlightening to the mind and ennobling to the heart; faithful and complete, as well as useful and practical.

Sophia Institute gratefully recognizes the Solidarity Association for preserving and encouraging the growth of our apostolate over the course of many years. Without their generous and timely support, this book would not be in your hands.

www.SophiaInstitute.com
www.CatholicExchange.com
www.CrisisMagazine.com
www.SophiaInstituteforTeachers.org